The GIANT Book of TRICKS and PUZZLES

Editor: Jacqui Bailey
Design: Millions Design
Illustrations: Peter Stephenson/*Jillian Burgess
Agency*, Millions Design

Produced by Grisewood & Dempsey Ltd.,
and exclusively distributed under the
Piccolo imprint by Pan Books Ltd.,
18–21 Cavaye Place, London SW10 9PG.

ISBN 0 330 29998 0
9 8 7 6 5 4 3 2 1
Printed in Yugoslavia

The GIANT Book of TRIICKS and PUZZLES

PETER ELDIN

A Piccolo Book

CONTENTS

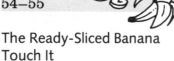

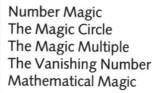

ABOUT THIS BOOK

I t is fun to fool people with tricks and puzzles, and there are enough ideas in this book to keep you funning and fooling for a long time to come. But do not show them to people just to prove how clever you are. People do not like to be put down so you should only do the tricks because you enjoy doing them and because you want other people to enjoy them as well.

Before you start, read through the tips and advice on this page.

PRACTICE MAKES PERFECT

Always try out your tricks in private first. It can be most embarrassing when a trick goes wrong simply because you have not tested it out for yourself. Some of the stunts in this book require a special knack which may take a little time to attain. You will only gain this knack by practising the tricks to make sure that you can do them properly.

The magic tricks should be practised until you can do them perfectly. Keep practising until you can do the trick without thinking. With some of the tricks you will find it useful to practise them in front of a mirror so you can spot any mistakes you might make from your audience's point of view.

The more you practise the better you will become – so keep at it. Only when you are confident you can do the trick well should you show it to anyone else.

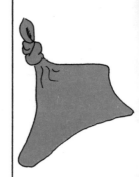

PATTER POINTS

Magicians and other performers call the talking they do 'patter'. Patter is important – sometimes the complete trick can depend on the way something is said. This is particularly true of lots of puzzles.

It is therefore a good idea to work out what you are going to say before you show anyone a trick. This does not mean that you have to write out a full script, but you should rehearse the important bits of your patter.

During your practice sessions talk out loud to an imaginary audience. In that way you will learn your patter

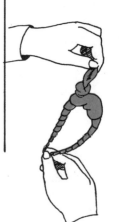

and the trick at the same time so the two will tie together quite naturally.

INVOLVING OTHER PEOPLE

Use your audience as part of your performance whenever possible. People like to be involved – so involve them. This can be done quite simply by borrowing some of the things you need for a trick. If you need a coin or a handkerchief ask someone if you can use theirs – but have your own ready, just in case your friends are broke, or the hanky needs washing!

IN GENERAL

Before showing a trick or a puzzle make sure you have everything you need. It is most embarrassing to get half-way through a trick and then to realize that you need a pencil, or a pack of cards, or whatever and there is not one available.

Never show a trick more than once on the same occasion. Some people, if you have fooled them with a trick, will ask you to do it again. Resist the temptation to do so for they are only trying to find out how you did it.

Never tell anyone how the tricks are done. Keep the secret to yourself.

If a trick goes wrong do not worry about it. Go on quickly to another trick. Later in the day try to see why the trick did not work (perhaps you hadn't practised enough) and see what you need to do to stop that mistake happening again.

DON'T GO ON

As a general rule, you will find that if you are enjoying yourself presenting these tricks then your friends will enjoy watching you. But you must learn when to stop. Don't keep on showing trick after trick for ages because you will end up boring your audience and they will steer clear of you in the future!

Just show a few tricks at a time and follow the old show business saying of 'always leave them asking for more'.

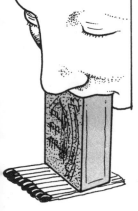

MAKE A PAPER CUP

handy to know how to make a cup from a sheet of paper.

Fold the square of paper in half diagonally, to bring corner D up to meet corner A (1).

Next, fold corner C across to touch the opposite edge (2) so it looks like the picture (3).

Turn the paper over and fold corner B across to the opposite edge, exactly like the last fold. Your paper should now look like diagram 4.

Fold A and D down on opposite sides of the paper and tuck them into the little pockets made by the previous fold (4). Open out the top and your cup is complete (5).

If you fold the bottom corners in a little the cup will stand on its own.

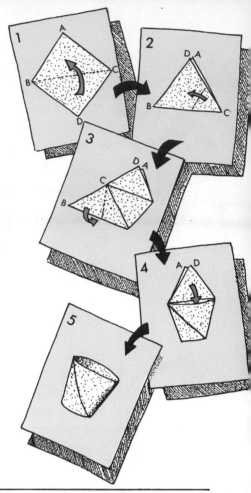

YOU NEED:
● A square sheet of fairly stiff paper, about 20 cm square

If you are ever out on a picnic, or on safari deep in darkest Mongolia, you will find it

IMPOSSIBLE TEAR

YOU NEED:
● A strip of paper

Take the strip of paper and make two tears in it so it looks something like the paper in the drawing.

Your victim, who has been watching you do this, will be wondering what you are up to. Now you spring the trap. "I bet you can't take this paper, with one end in each hand, and pull it apart into three pieces."

As the tears are both the same length, your friend will probably take up your challenge. But when he or she pulls the paper only one end comes free!

Strange as it may sound, it

is impossible to tear the strip into three pieces. The original tears can be made almost to the opposite edge but still only one piece comes off. Try it and see.

NOTHING IS IMPOSSIBLE

Nothing is impossible – especially if you cheat!

Supposing someone asks you to do the 'Impossible Tear'? You know you cannot accept the challenge because the feat is impossible. So, what do you do? You accept the challenge!

Take the paper, one end in each hand and start tearing. Your friend will think you have been caught – but then you lift the paper up to your mouth and hold the centre portion between your lips. It is now an easy matter to tear the strip into three!

10

Pieces Of Eight

YOU NEED:
- A square piece of paper
- Scissors

Hand your friend the paper and pair of scissors. Challenge her to cut an octagon shape from the paper. To do this she is not allowed to use a pencil, ruler, compasses or anything else other than the scissors.

Unless your friend has sneaked a look at this book it is very unlikely that she will be able to do it. It is, however, quite easy to do – when you know the answer!

Take the square of paper and, using the letters shown in the diagram, make the following moves.

Fold the edge AC down on to FH and make a crease before opening the paper out again. Now fold it in half the other way so that the edge AF meets CH. Open the paper out once again and you will see that the creases you have made give you the location of the centre of each side (marked B, D, E and G in the diagram).

Next fold down the four corners along the imaginary lines DB, GE, BE and DG. Open up the paper again and the creases you have made will mark out the square DBGE.

Just a few more folds to go! First fold the edge from C to E down to meet the line BE. Open the paper, fold BC down to BE and open the paper again. These last two folds will form the lines BI and EI.

Repeat the last two folds at each of the other three corners and the octagon will be marked out clearly in creases and can easily be cut out with scissors.

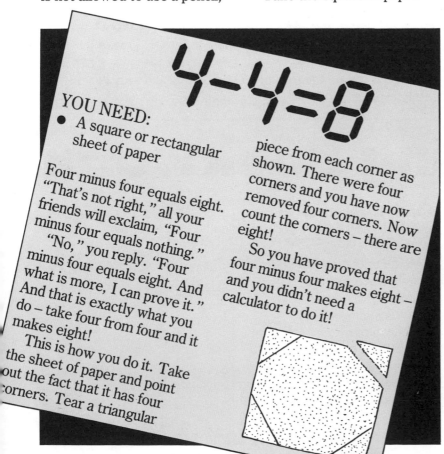

YOU NEED:
- A square or rectangular sheet of paper

Four minus four equals eight. "That's not right," all your friends will exclaim, "Four minus four equals nothing."

"No," you reply. "Four minus four equals eight. And what is more, I can prove it." And that is exactly what you do – take four from four and it makes eight!

This is how you do it. Take the sheet of paper and point out the fact that it has four corners. Tear a triangular piece from each corner as shown. There were four corners and you have now removed four corners. Now count the corners – there are eight!

So you have proved that four minus four makes eight – and you didn't need a calculator to do it!

A PAPER PUZZLE

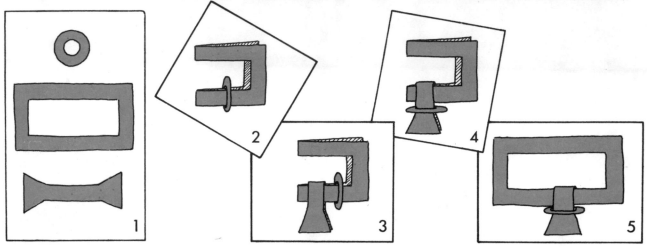

YOU NEED:
- A sheet of card
- Scissors

Cut these three shapes from the card (1). Bend the rectangle in half. Do this very carefully for you must not crease the card. Now place the ring over the bottom bars of the rectangle as shown (2).

Take the bow-shaped card and fold it in half. Push one half of this piece in-between the bottom bars so it hangs on one side only (3). You may need to slide the ring up the side of the rectangle to make this easier.

Now bring the ring back along the bars and over the top of the folded bow (4).

Open out the rectangle and the three pieces are now joined together as shown (5).

Hand the cards to a friend and challenge him or her to remove the ring without tearing anything. When your friend gives up, you do it just by reversing the movements you made to put the whole thing together. Do not let anyone else see exactly how you do this and they will be completely baffled.

Burrowing Bookworm

Billy the bookworm loves books. He particularly likes burrowing in them.

All the books shown on this bookshelf are 5 cm in thickness. Plus, each cover has a thickness of $\frac{1}{4}$ cm.

If Billy burrows in a straight line from the first page of 'Growing Old' to the last page of 'Fighting Crime' how far does he burrow?

The answer is on page 125.

12

YOU NEED:
- An old book, the thicker the better
- Glue

Glue the pages of your book together (so make sure that it *is* an old book!). There is no need to put glue in the centre of the pages – just around the edges will do.

When the glue has set, ask an adult to cut out the centre part of the pages so the book looks like the one shown in the picture.

You now have an excellent hiding place for all your money, jewellery, secret messages and so on. Just put your valuable things into the hole and then close the book. When you put the book on a bookshelf, along with all your other books, no one will ever know about this secret hiding place.

This is a very handy thing for secret agents as it is particularly useful for concealing secret messages, coded information, disguises, microfilm, or bombs!

A Book With A Secret

YOU NEED:
- A large book
- A paper bag

Get the largest book you can find and stand it upright on a table. Now challenge your friends to blow it over.

When they have had a go and are completely breathless you show them how it can be done.

Stand the book on a paper bag, with the neck of the bag hanging over the edge of the table. Now blow into the bag and the book will topple over. Such is the power of your strong breath!

Invulnerable String

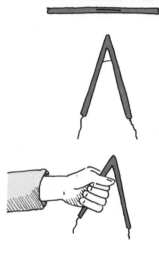

YOU NEED:
- A waxed paper drinking straw
- A piece of string
- Scissors

Here is a neat magic trick you can try. You show the straw and the string to your friends and thread the string through the straw. Then you bend the straw at the centre.

Now you cut through the straw at the centre. It is obvious to everyone watching that you must have cut through the string also, but when you pull it from the two halves of the straw it is completely unharmed!

What you do not tell your friends is that you did some secret preparation before you showed the trick. What you do is to cut a short slit along the centre section of the straw. When you show the straw to your audience be careful that no one sees this slit.

Thread the string through the straw and then bend the straw in half. A slight tug on the ends of the string is enough to pull it through the slit. Your audience do not see this because it is covered by your finger and thumb.

You now cut through the centre of the straw, make a few magic passes, then pull out the string 'completely restored'.

Drop Them In

YOU NEED:
- A few drinking straws
- An empty bottle

With just a few drinking straws and an empty bottle you and your friends can play a great game.

First cut the straws into short pieces, each piece being about 3 cm long. Place the bottle on the floor.

You and your fellow players now take it in turns to stand over the bottle and try to drop the straws in it.

When the first person has used up all the straws, count up how many he or she managed to get into the bottle and then let another player have a go. The person who gets the most straws in the bottle is declared the winner.

STRAWS FOR APPLAUSE

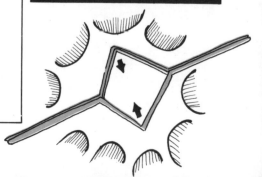

Flatten two paper straws, then bend them and place them together as shown in the illustration.

When the ends are jerked apart the centre sections are straightened, so they hit each other with a sharp clapping noise.

By moving your hands in and out quickly you can make quite a racket!

STICKY FINGERS

YOU NEED:

● A drinking straw

Your friends will think you are a real magician when you make an ordinary straw stick to your hand. It looks like real magic.

This is how you do it. Take the straw in your left hand. Now grasp your left wrist with your right hand. Secretly straighten your right fore-finger so it can hold the straw against the palm of your other hand. Open out the fingers of your left hand and the straw will seem to have a magnetic attraction to your hand.

Only show this trick with the back of your left hand towards your audience. If you ever accidentally turn and show the other side of your hand everyone will see how the trick is done.

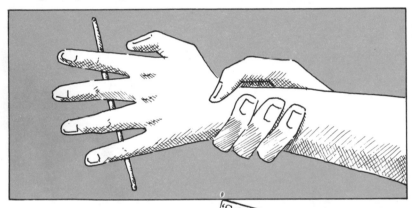

The Last Straw

'Sticky Fingers' is not an earth-shattering bit of magic. But you can make it quite amusing by going one step further – like this.

Do the trick in the normal way. Then say to your audience, "I'll let you into a secret – the straw is held in place by my thumb." As you say this you turn so that your left palm is facing the audience. At the same time you bring your left thumb down to hold the straw and move the right forefinger down and around the left wrist. The audience can now see that the straw is held in place by the left thumb.

Now turn again so that the back of the left hand is facing the audience once more. Bring the right forefinger back up to hold the straw and lift the left thumb into view as you say, "I mustn't wiggle my thumb or I will drop the straw." You wiggle your left thumb, but the straw remains stuck to your hand!

Now place the straw on a table and then make magic passes over and around it. Much to everyone's surprise the straw begins to roll away from you, following the movement of your hand across the table.

THE ROLLING STRAW

The secret of this trick is amazingly simple. A lot of people will think you have a thread attached to your hand and the straw – but it is not as complicated as that! All you have to do is blow the straw across the table!

The movements of your hands around and then away from the straw are simply to make everyone look at the table so that no one will see you blowing.

15

TURN THE TRIANGLE

YOU NEED:
- Ten coins

Arrange the coins on a table in a triangular formation as shown.

The triangle is pointing upwards. By moving just three of the coins can you change the arrangement so that the triangle is pointing downwards?

The answer is on page 125.

HEADS AND TAILS

YOU NEED:
- Sixteen coins

Arrange the coins in a square so that the coins alternate heads and tails, like those shown here (1).

Can you now rearrange the coins so that each horizontal row consists of four coins that are all the same way, as shown in the next picture (2)? To do this you are allowed to touch only two coins and make just one move!

The answer is on page 125.

COUNT THE COINS

YOU NEED:
- Six coins

Place the coins on a table so they form the shape of a letter L – with four coins forming a vertical column and three coins in a horizontal row.

Can you now, by moving just one coin, arrange the coins so it is possible to count four coins both vertically and horizontally?

The answer is on page 125.

THE THREE COIN TRICK

YOU NEED:
- Three coins

Place the coins on the table as shown, with two of the coins touching and the third a short distance away.

Now challenge a friend to get the separate coin (C) in-between the other two coins (A and B). To do this your friend must not touch the coin marked A and he must not move coin B.

When your friend gives up (and he certainly will!), you show how it is done. All you have to do is place the tip of your left forefinger on coin B then use the right fingers to knock coin C sharply against coin B.

This knock will cause coin A to move away to the left so it is now an easy matter to push coin C between A and B.

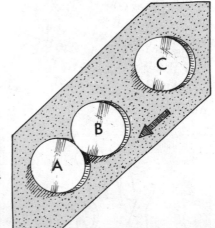

THE THREE COIN TRICK 2

Place three coins in a row on the table. Can you now get the middle coin out of the central position without touching it?

The solution to this problem is really quite simple but your friends will be very puzzled.

All you have to do is move a coin from one end of the row and place it at the other end of the row. The original middle coin is now no longer in the middle. Easy when you know how, isn't it?

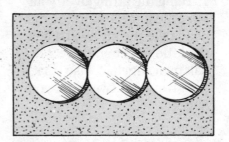

YOU NEED:
- A coin
- A sheet of plain paper
- A pencil

Show your friends the coin and sheet of paper. While your back is turned one of your friends hides the coin under the paper.

Without looking beneath the paper you can now tell them which way up the coin is.

How? All you do is run the point of a pencil over the paper where the coin is hidden. You will soon be able to see an impression of the coin on the paper and you can see whether it is heads or tails uppermost!

WHICH WAY UP?

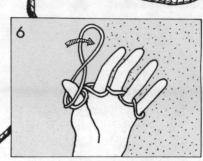

SLIPPERY STRING

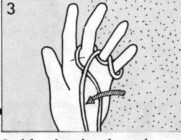

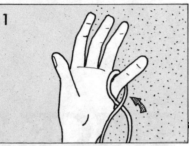

1. Hang the string over your left little finger. With the right hand take the string just below the little finger and give it a half turn anticlockwise (that's the string you twist, not your finger!).

3. After looping the string over the middle finger give the string a half turn, this time anticlockwise.

6. Having threaded all your fingers together one way you now do the same in the opposite direction. Place the loop back over your thumb and give the string a half turn anticlockwise.

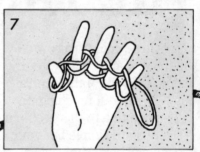

2. Now loop the next portion of string over the third finger of your left hand. Give the string another half turn, clockwise this time.

4. Put the loop over the index finger and then give the string a full turn clockwise (not a half turn this time).

7. Carry on looping the string around the remaining fingers giving a half turn each time, first one way and then the other, until your hand is completely entangled in the string.

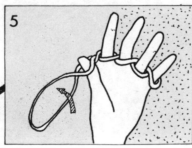

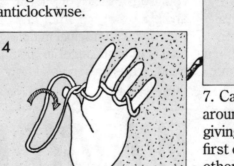

5. Now there is only the thumb (unless you come from Mars). Put your thumb into the loop and give the string a half turn anticlockwise.

8. Get someone to hold the tips of each of your four fingers (not the thumb). Slip the thumb from its loops, pull on the string with your right hand and the string will appear to pass through your fingers.

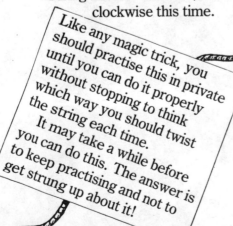

ALL TIED UP

YOU NEED:
- A length of soft rope or string
- A thick elastic band
- A ball-point pen

You hand someone the rope and ask for one end of it to be tied around your right wrist. The other end of the rope is tied around your left wrist (1).

Now show everyone the elastic band and ball-point pen. Ask someone to write something on the band so that you cannot change it for another without everyone knowing.

You now turn your back for a second or two. When you turn around again the band is threaded on the centre of the rope between your wrists. Someone checks the writing on the band and it is obvious that it is the same band that was shown earlier.

Once again you turn your back for a short while. This time when you turn back round the band is free of the rope. It is still the same elastic band, it is completely unharmed and your wrists are still tied securely.

You did not have time to undo the rope and tie it up again while your back was turned so how did you do it?

This is what you do when your back is turned.

Slip the rubber band over your left hand. Then push the band under the loop of rope that is around your wrist (2).

Pull the band through completely. It is now still around your wrist, but it is under the tied loop (3).

Bring the band up and over the left hand so it is threaded on to the rope (4). Now you can turn back to face your audience.

To remove the band simply do all the above movements in the reverse order.

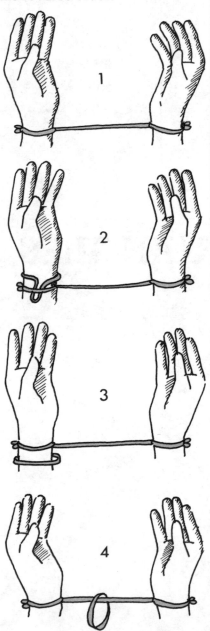

UNDER THE CUP

YOU NEED:
- A cup
- A coin

Place the cup mouth-down on a table. Next to the cup place the coin.

Can you now get the coin under the cup? To do this you are allowed to touch only the coin. You must not touch the cup in any way, nor must anyone or anything else be used to move the cup.

Give up? All you have to do is pick up the coin and then hold it under the table directly beneath the cup. It is now under the cup!

Try this on your friends and see how many of them can manage to solve the problem before you explain to them how it is done.

19

QUICK
ON THE
DRAW

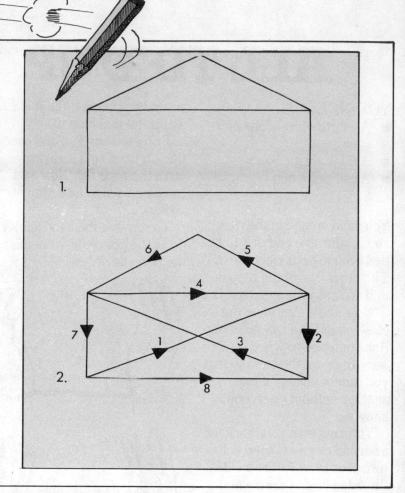

YOU NEED:
- A sheet of drawing paper
- A pencil

Anyone can draw an envelope like this (1). But can you draw it in one complete sequence without lifting your pen or pencil from the paper and without going over any line more than once? That's not so easy, is it?

The answer is to start at the bottom-left corner and then draw the lines in the sequence shown (2).

TRICKY TRIANGLES

YOU NEED:
- A sheet of drawing paper
- A pen or pencil

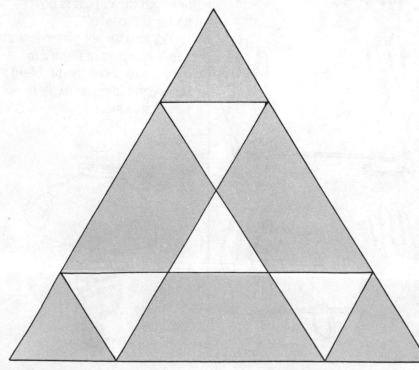

Here is a picture of some tricky triangles. Can you copy this design on to a sheet of paper without lifting your pencil (or pen) off the paper and without going over any line twice? And, just to make it even more difficult, you are not allowed to cross over any line that you have already drawn!

When you have managed to do that (without looking up the answer) see if you can say how many triangles there are in the drawing.

The answer is on page 126.

ANOTHER TRIANGLE TEASER

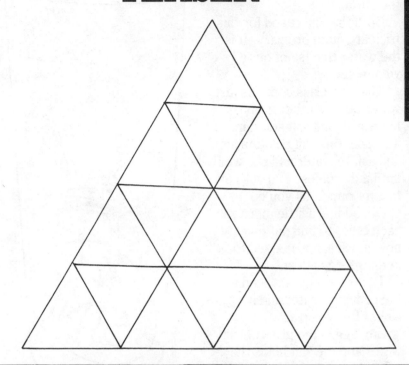

Here is another triangle of triangles to tax your wits and your drawing ability.

See if you can draw this diagram without lifting your pen or pencil from the paper and without going over any line twice.

The answer is on page 126.

ENIGMATIC EMBLEM

YOU NEED:
- Paper and pencil

This emblem is the badge of the Ancient Order of Prehistoric Prestidigitators. This society is so secret that no one is allowed in.

As there is absolutely no chance of your becoming a member perhaps you would like to try a puzzle using the emblem. See if you can draw it without taking your pen or pencil off the paper and without going over any line more than once.

The answer is on page 126.

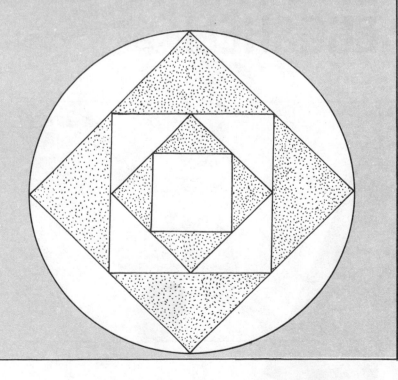

SINK
OR
SWIM

YOU NEED:
- Two hard-boiled eggs
- A felt-tip pen
- Two glasses of water
- Salt

You hand a friend the eggs and the felt-tip pen. Ask your friend to write the word 'sink' on one egg and the word 'swim' on the other.

You then take the 'sink' egg and place it in a glass of water. The egg sinks to the bottom. What else would you expect?

The 'swim' egg is then placed in another glass of water and it floats just below the surface!

Both the eggs used for this trick are quite ordinary. It is the water that is not quite what it seems.

The first glass contains just water but the other glass holds a strong salt solution. To make this salt solution just add salt to water and stir well until it dissolves. You will have to experiment as you go along, adding a little more salt each time, to find out exactly how much salt is needed to keep the egg afloat.

The 'sink' egg is placed in the ordinary water and it sinks. But you place the 'swim' egg in the glass of salt water and the salt holds the egg up near the surface.

SPIN THE
EGGSHELL

YOU NEED:
- An eggshell
- A broad-rimmed dinner plate

Next time you have a boiled egg for your breakfast keep the shell for this amazing stunt.

Wet the rim of the dinner plate with water. Put the half eggshell on the moistened rim and then tilt the plate slightly. The shell will naturally slide down the side of the plate – but much to everyone's surprise the eggshell will spin rapidly as it slides down.

If you keep turning your hand you should be able to keep the egg spinning on the plate for quite some time.

To really show off you could cut the shape of a dancer from a piece of card and, by means of two slits in the base of the card, attach it to the eggshell, then make it pirouette.

EGGSELLENT BALANCE

YOU NEED:
- Two forks
- A bottle cork
- One hard-boiled egg
- An empty bottle

Push a fork into each side of the cork so that the forks hang downwards as shown. Using this peculiar device you will now find that you can balance an egg on the rim of a bottle, exactly as shown in the picture.

It serves no useful purpose but it does look rather amazing. You could, if you like, present it as a puzzle by first handing someone an egg and a bottle and challenging them to balance the egg on the bottle's rim. It is only after your friend gives up the task that you bring forth the cork and the two forks that will enable you to succeed where your friend has failed.

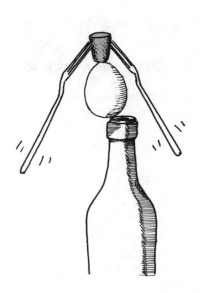

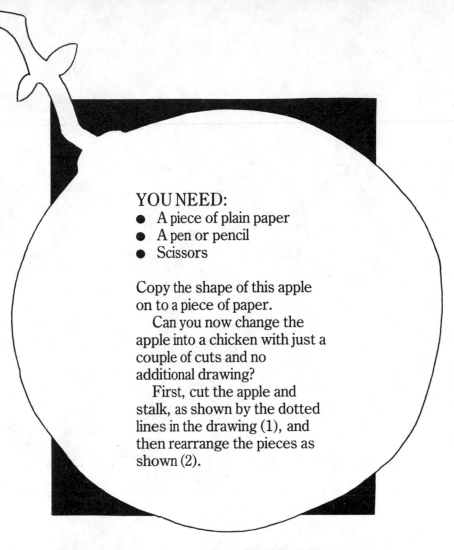

YOU NEED:
- A piece of plain paper
- A pen or pencil
- Scissors

Copy the shape of this apple on to a piece of paper.

Can you now change the apple into a chicken with just a couple of cuts and no additional drawing?

First, cut the apple and stalk, as shown by the dotted lines in the drawing (1), and then rearrange the pieces as shown (2).

PIPPIN CHICKEN

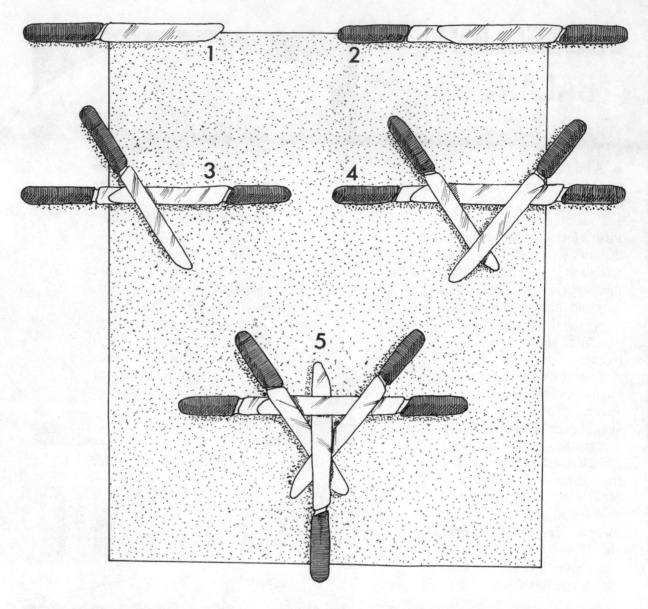

KNIFE PATTERN

YOU NEED:
- Five ordinary table knives (long-bladed are best)

Place four of the knives on a table. Now, can you lift those knives using only the fifth knife?

Before reading the answer, get five knives (not sharp ones) and see if you can do it. This will give you an idea of how difficult it is before you challenge your friends to have a go.

To accomplish this seemingly impossible feat this is what you do.

Place one knife on the table (1). Easy so far, isn't it! Now place the second knife so that its blade overlaps the first (2).

The third knife is placed at an angle across the first two (3). And the fourth is used to form a triangular shape (4).

Now comes the tricky part. Take the fifth knife and push it over the blades of the third and fourth knives and under knives one and two (5). Take hold of the handle of the fifth knife and lift. With a bit of luck you should be able to lift all the other four knives at the same time.

MAKE A PAPER ALTAR

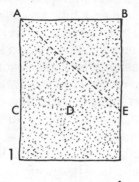

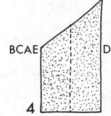

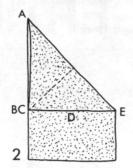

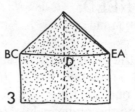

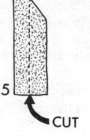

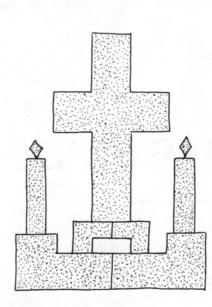

CUT

YOU NEED:
- A rectangular sheet of paper
- Scissors

Can you take a sheet of paper and cut out the shape of a church altar, complete with lighted candles and a cross?

That sounds reasonably straightforward, although the lighted candles might cause a bit of a problem! Actually, there is a further complication that has not yet been mentioned – you are allowed to cut the paper only once and

that cut has to be a single, straight cut.

That is not so easy, is it! But, of course, it can be done – and this is how you do it.
1. Take the sheet of paper and fold one corner down to meet the opposite edge. If you look at the diagram this corner is marked B and you have to fold it down to touch point C.
2. Next, fold corner A down to point E.
3. Now fold the paper in half lengthways by folding side EA on to side BC.
4. Having done that, fold the

paper in half again (by folding D on to BCAE).
5. Cut the paper in half lengthways with a single, straight cut and you will end up with nine separate pieces. These pieces can be laid out as shown in the last picture to form the altar, candles and cross.

When opening out the pieces of paper, form the altar first. Then put the candles in position. Now put the 'flames' on the candles. Save the opening of the cross until last as this is quite spectacular.

25

BALANCED ON A FINGERTIP

YOU NEED:

● Ten small coins

Place the coins on the table. Can you now take five of the coins, one at a time, and place them on the fingernails of your left hand, one coin on each nail?

That was easy, wasn't it! Now comes the difficult bit. Keeping those coins on the nails of the left hand can you place the remaining five coins on the nails of the right hand,

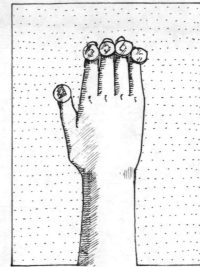

without dropping any of the ten coins!

That is not quite so easy and it may take you quite a bit of practice to do it every time. You will find the feat a lot easier if the coins destined to go on the right hand are first arranged in a row along the edge of the table. You will then discover that it is relatively easy for the left hand (still balancing the coins on the finger nails) to slide the coins, one at a time, from the table and on to the fingers of the right hand.

If you challenge your friends to attempt this feat you do not of course tell them of this little tip!

TWO LITTLE BIRDS

YOU NEED:

● Two small pieces of paper

This is a good way of amusing very young children. Stick a small piece of paper on the nail of the middle finger of each hand. (If you lick your finger, or the paper a little, this should do.) Rest these fingers on the edge of the table and then recite this little rhyme with the following actions:

"Two little birds, sitting on a wall." Wiggle the two fingers slightly.

"One named Peter . . ." Lift the right hand a short way off the table and then replace it.

"One named Paul." Lift the left hand from the table and then replace it.

"Fly away Peter . . ." Lift the right hand and quickly bend your right second finger into the palm. At the same time extend the right forefinger and then bring the hand back down to the table.

"Fly away Paul . . ." Repeat the last action with your left hand.

"Come back Peter . . ." Raise the right hand and return it to the table, changing from the forefinger to the second finger as you do so.

"Come back Paul." Repeat the last action with your left hand.

Not a great mystery but you will find that young children really enjoy it.

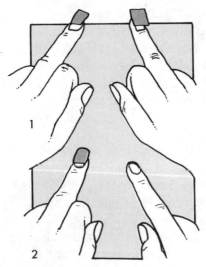

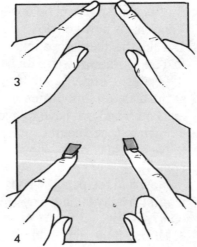

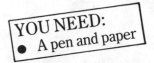

SUM IT UP

Write these numbers on a piece of paper:

Now challenge someone to choose any six digits from the 15 digits shown and write them down, one under the other, so that they add up to a total of 21.

The column of figures they use must be made up of single digits only. In other words you cannot put two together (such as 1 and 5 to make 15). The six chosen digits must form a single column and they must total 21.

If you try this yourself you will find that it just cannot be done. So your friends will have to give up sooner or later.

When everyone admits defeat you demonstrate how to do it. How can you do that when it is actually impossible? This is how.

Write down the three 1s. Underneath these put the three 9s – like this:

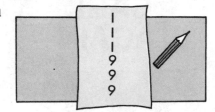

If you add this up you will see that it totals 30 – but this is where the sneaky bit comes in. Turn the paper over – the 9s become 6s – and the column of figures now adds up to 21!

ANSWER IN ADVANCE

YOU NEED:
- A pen and paper
- A calculator may be useful

First write the number 9 on a sheet of paper. Fold the paper, without letting anyone see what you have written, and place it on the table in full view.

Now ask someone to say any number between 10 and 98, except double numbers, such as 11, 22, 33 and so on. Let us suppose they pick 25. Write this down, or put it into your calculator.

The number is now reversed. (In our example 25 reversed gives 52). Now subtract the smaller number

from the larger number (52 − 25 = 27).

The answer (27) is now divided by the difference between the digits of the original number. This may sound a bit complicated but if you take a look at the number in our example (25) you will see that it is not really difficult. In the example the difference between the two digits is three (5 − 2 = 3). Divide 27 by 3 and the answer is 9.

Ask someone to open the paper that has been on view all the time. On it is written the number 9 – you knew that answer even before the sum was started!

In fact the answer is always 9 – but there is no need to tell your friends that! Here is another example.

State any number between
10 and 98   94
Reverse it   49
Take the smaller number
from the larger   45
Divide this answer by the
difference in the digits of the
number you first thought of:
9 − 4 = 5, 45 ÷ 5 = 9.

And the answer is 9!

27

YOUR CARD

YOU NEED:
- A pack of cards

Tell your friends that you are an expert magician and that you are going to show them an

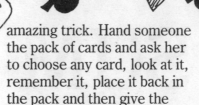

amazing trick. Hand someone the pack of cards and ask her to choose any card, look at it, remember it, place it back in the pack and then give the cards a good shuffle.

You now say, "I am such a fantastically brilliant magician I bet I can hand you your chosen card even though the pack has been thoroughly shuffled."

Take the pack and remove

any card face down. Your friend will think that this is her card.

Ask your friend what card she chose. As soon as she tells you, place the card you are holding back in the pack and hand the complete pack to your friend. You have now handed her the chosen card just as you said you would – it must be in the pack somewhere!

After showing someone 'Your Card' you then offer to do the trick properly, saying that this time you really will hand the person their selected card.

Once again a card is chosen and shuffled back into the pack. Again you offer to find the chosen card and you take out one card (any card) face down. This time the person who chose the card really will think that you have managed to find it and that you were just joking the first time.

YOUR CARD AGAIN

Ask the person what card they chose. You then put the card you are holding back into the pack (unless it happens to be the one just named – in which case you show it and take the credit for being a brilliant magician). Now run through the cards and take out the card just named and hand it to the person concerned.

Once again you have done just what you said you would do – you have handed your friend his chosen card!

YOUR CARD FOR REAL

If you plan to show your friends 'Your Card' and 'Your Card – Again' it is a good idea to be able to do a proper card trick. Here is one you can try.

Have the cards shuffled and then ask someone to take any

card from the pack. Get them to show the card to everyone else present. While they are doing this take a quick peep at the bottom card of the pack. You must remember this card.

Ask the person who is helping you to put his card back, face down, on the top of the pack. You now cut the cards into two halves and put the top half underneath what was the bottom half. The chosen card is now buried in the centre of the pack (it is actually underneath the card you saw on the bottom). Cut the cards a few more times

until everyone is convinced that the chosen card is completely lost.

Now you can tell everyone that you really are a great magician and that you can find the chosen card. Spread the cards out in front of you and look for the card you saw on the bottom of the pack earlier. The person's chosen card will be to the right of the card you saw so all you have to do is take it from the pack. Ask for the name of the chosen card and then show the one you are holding – this time you are absolutely right!

28

Floating Corks

YOU NEED:
- A bowl of water
- Seven bottle corks

Drop the corks in the water and tell your friends that corks always float on their sides. They will be able to see that this is true for all the corks will be floating on their sides.

You now challenge your friends to make the corks float upright. Now matter how often the corks are placed in the water in an upright position they will steadfastly refuse to float that way up – until you demonstrate how it can be done.

You take all seven corks out of the water and then hold them all together, so there is one cork in the centre of the group surrounded by the other six corks. Holding them bunched together, immerse them all in the water in an upright position. Now allow them to come to the surface of the water and then gradually release your grip – and, wonder of wonders, the corks will remain floating upright! You are so clever!

CORK bOUnce

If you drop a cork on to the floor or a table it will invariably fall over and settle on its side.

Challenge your friends to drop a cork so that it stands on end. Needless to say, they cannot do it – but you can. The secret is to drop the cork so that it falls on its side. In most cases the cork will then bounce up off the surface and stand on its end.

Cork In The Middle

YOU NEED:
- A glass of water
- A small bottle cork

Drop the cork into the glass of water. Can you now make the cork float in the middle of the surface of the water?

For some reason the cork will refuse to stay in the centre, but there is a simple method to make it do just that. Fill the glass right up to the brim. The cork will now float in the centre due to the fact that the surface of the water is at a slightly higher level at the centre than it is around the rim of the glass.

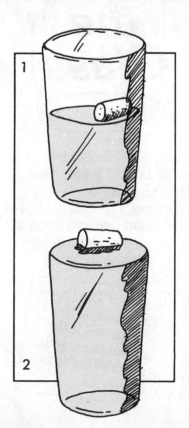

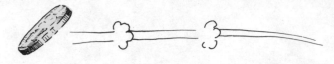

Off the Glass

1

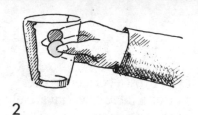

2

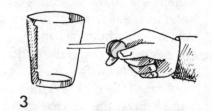

3

The problem now is how to get both these two coins between your finger and thumb. In doing this, one coin is to be touched only by the thumb and only the forefinger is allowed to touch the other coin.

The answer to the problem is to move both coins at the same time. You place your thumb on one coin, your forefinger on the other and then slide them down the sides of the glass as shown in the illustration.

When you get near to the bottom of the glass move your hand in towards your body so the coins slide off the glass, then snap them together between finger and thumb.

YOU NEED:
- Two coins
- A glass tumbler

Balance the coins on opposite sides of the tumbler's rim, as shown in the picture.

On the Glass

With a little bit of practice you will find that it is possible to do 'Off The Glass' in reverse.

Balance a coin on the ball of your thumb and another coin on the tip of your forefinger. Now approach the glass

tumbler and gently slap the coins against each side of the glass at the bottom. You can now slide the coins up the side of the glass. Now comes the difficult bit, for you have to manoeuvre the coins until they are balanced on the rim. This calls for some patience and a steady hand, but it can be done.

When you have practised this so you can do it every time, you can show your friends the coins and the glass and challenge them to balance the coins on the rim. To do this they are allowed to touch one coin with the thumb only and the other coin with the forefinger only.

This is quite a difficult problem to solve so you will be able to show how clever you are by actually doing it as described above.

Do not show 'Off The Glass' and 'On The Glass' at the same time. One will baffle your friends but the solution may give them a clue as to how to do the other.

Get the Coin

YOU NEED:
- Two large coins and one smaller, thinner coin
- A glass tumbler

Place the two larger coins on the table a little way apart with the smaller coin between them. Make sure the table has a tablecloth on it. Now turn the glass over and balance it on top of the two large coins.

The problem you now put to the people watching you is, "Can you get the small coin out from beneath the glass without touching the glass or any of the coins?"

This really is quite a problem and it is bound to get your audience guessing. When they admit that they cannot work out the answer you simply start scratching the tablecloth a short distance away from the glass. Much to everyone's surprise the small coin crawls out from beneath the glass all by itself!

YOU NEED:
- A large coin (50 pence piece)
- An empty bottle
- A flat-bladed kitchen knife

Place the coin on a table. Now balance the bottle upside down on top of the coin.

Can you get the coin out from under the bottle without touching the bottle, and without anyone or anything else touching the bottle?

Think about it for a moment . . . it is not going to be easy, is it? In fact the solution is quite simple. Take the knife and hit the coin sharply with the blade. The blade knocks the coin out of the way and

Out From Under

actually passes under the neck of the bottle before the bottle falls to the table-top. (If you can find one, try practising with a plastic bottle first.)

LINE THEM UP

YOU NEED:
- A pencil and paper
- Three coins

Draw a straight line on the sheet of paper. Place the paper and three coins on a table. Now challenge someone to put the coins on the paper in such a way that there are two heads on one side of the line and two tails on the other side of the line.

Sounds impossible doesn't it? But, of course, it is not impossible, although your friends will think it is when they try to do it.

In fact there is a bit of a catch to the solution. All you have to do is place one coin, head uppermost, on one side of the line. A second coin, with its tail side showing, is

placed on the other side of the line. Then stand the third coin on its edge actually on the line.

There are now two heads on one side of the line and two tails on the other – just the way you wanted!

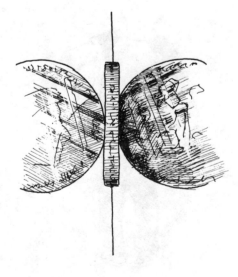

FINGERS AGAINST FISTS

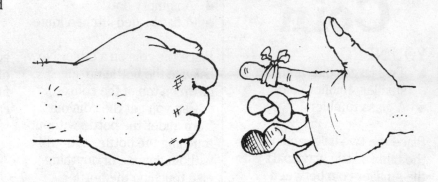

Ask someone to form their hands into two fists and to place one fist on top of the other. Tell your friend to hold his fists tightly together for you are about to test his strength. And, what is more, you are going to use only one finger of each hand to prove that you are stronger than your friend.

You then make a fist keeping the index finger of each hand pointing outwards. Swing your hands together, hitting the back of both your friend's fists with your index fingers as hard as you can. Much to his surprise (and maybe to yours as well) his fists will separate.

This is easy to do because your friend will be exerting an up and down pressure to keep his fists together. This makes it much easier for your sideways attack to succeed.

FISTS AGAINST FINGERS

If someone should challenge you to the test described in 'Fingers Against Fists' accept the challenge – for your friend will not be able to win.

As you put your fists together put the thumb of the lower hand into the upper hand. Do not let your friend see you do this.

With your upper hand grasping the lower thumb your fists will be linked firmly together and your opponent will never manage to knock them apart.

STRONG ARM

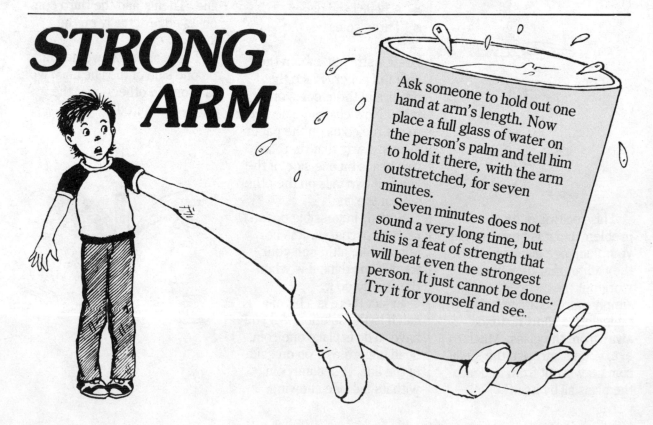

Ask someone to hold out one hand at arm's length. Now place a full glass of water on the person's palm and tell him to hold it there, with the arm outstretched, for seven minutes.

Seven minutes does not sound a very long time, but this is a feat of strength that will beat even the strongest person. It just cannot be done. Try it for yourself and see.

NOSE IN THE GLASS

"Can you drink a glass of water without putting your nose in the glass?" This is the challenge you issue to your friends. When they try, they spill water all over the place,

your mouth. You can use a straw. Cleverest of all is this final technique. You actually drink from the glass – but from the opposite side to normal. You will have to

no matter how hard they try.

In fact there are several ways you can do this without spilling any of the liquid.

You can use a spoon to lift the liquid from the glass to

practise this in private until you can do it without spilling any of the water. But the important point is that your nose is most definitely outside the glass.

Arm Up

You are the strongest person you know – and, what is more, you can prove it!

Place the palm of one hand flat on top of your head. Now challenge the strongest person available to grasp your forearm and, by pushing from below, try to lift your hand from your head.

Unless you are an absolute weakling and your friend is weight-lifting champion of the world it is very unlikely that he or she will be able to do it.

PAPER STRENGTH

YOU NEED:
- A paper napkin

Roll the napkin into a tight roll. Then twist the roll a little to make it even tighter.

Get a friend to hold the roll, with one end in each hand. Now ask him or her to pull on the roll and tear it in two.

If you try this for yourself you will discover that you have to have muscles on your muscles in order to do it. So it will be no surprise to you when your friend has to give up the challenge.

You now bet your friend that you can do it. No doubt your friend will have seen you do many other impossible stunts (thanks to this book), but this one seems so impossible that it just cannot be true. As your friend has tried and failed everyone will expect you to fail as well. But you succeed because you cheat by putting some water on the centre of your roll. (If you can do this secretly, all to the better.) Leave it for a few seconds to allow the water to penetrate the paper and then you will find it a fairly easy job to pull the napkin apart.

GUESS THE PAGE

Ask someone to pick any book from a bookshelf and then to open it at any page while your back is turned. That person is then asked to place his hand on either the right or the left-hand page. A second person is then asked to place her hand on the other page.

You now ask the first person to multiply his page number by two. The second person is asked to multiply her page number by three. The two totals are then added together and you are told the answer.

As soon as you are told this figure you immediately reveal who is touching the right-hand page and who is touching the left-hand page.

How did you know? This is how. If the figure is even, the first person is touching the right page. If the figure is odd the first person is touching the left page.

This trick works because all books are printed with the even page numbers to the left and the odd page numbers to the right.

BOOK CATCH

This is a neat little stunt with which to impress your friends.

Place a book on a table so that it projects over the edge. Bring your hand up beneath the book so the back of your fingers strike it underneath. This will cause the book to revolve in the air. Your hand continues upwards and catches the opposite end of the book after it has made a half turn in the air.

The pictures show the complete action. You will have to practise this before showing it to anyone, but after a while you will find that you can even do this with a pack of cards, without the cards flying all around the room!

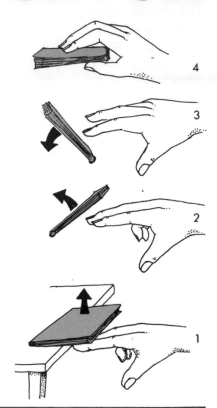

JUMP IT

Show someone a small book and say, "I bet that if I place this book on the floor you will not be able to jump over it."

As the book is so small your friend will think that it will be easy to jump over it.

You then place the book on the floor – in the corner of the room!

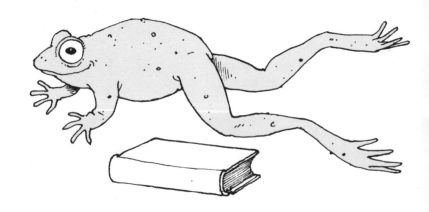

YOU NEED:
● A stick of coloured chalk

Secretly moisten your left thumb nail and then rub some coloured chalk on it. You are now ready to show your friends an amazing trick.

Show your left palm (be careful that no one sees the chalk on your thumb nail) and then place your hand under the table.

Your right hand now shows the stick of chalk and draws a short line on the table-top (so this is definitely not a trick to be performed on the dining-room table!). Now use the right palm to rub the mark off the table, but tell everyone watching that you are rubbing

THROUGH THE TABLE

the mark *through* the table.

At the same time, under the table, close your left hand into a fist with your thumb inside. This lets you run your thumb nail across your palm to put a chalk mark on your hand.

Bring your hand out from under the table, with your palm upwards, and it will seem to your friends that the chalk mark really has travelled through the table-top and on to your hand.

GUESS THE COLOUR

YOU NEED:
● A set of coloured felt-tip pens

Tell a friend that you will try to read her mind. Hand the pens to your friend and then turn your back. Put your hands out behind you and ask her to choose any colour, to hand you the pen of that colour and then to hide all the other pens.

You now turn back to face her and begin to concentrate as if trying to read her mind. With your hands still behind your back, secretly slip the top off the pen and make a mark on one of your fingers. Then put the top back on the pen.

Keeping the pen behind

your back you now bring your hand to your forehead as if thinking hard. As you bring the hand up to your face it is a simple matter to spot the mark on your finger (provided

you have remembered to use the correct hand!).

You can now announce what the chosen colour is and you will be regarded as a truly great mind-reader!

UNDER
THE
TABLE

YOU NEED:
- A die (one dice)

Your friends sit around a table. You sit on the floor, under the table. That may sound a strange thing to do but there is a reason – you are about to show an amazing magic trick.

On the table is a die and your friends are invited to throw it several times. Each time it is thrown you tell them what number is uppermost on the die, even though you are still under the table and cannot see it!

One of your friends seated at the table is your secret assistant. He sits casually with one hand resting on his knee. On each throw of the die he signals with his hand the number that has been thrown. One finger for One, two fingers for Two, three fingers for Three and so on up to Five. If a Six is thrown he closes his fist.

THE LONGEST WORD

YOU NEED:
- A pencil and paper

Hand someone a piece of paper and a pencil and say, "I bet I can write a longer word than you."

Your friend may even go to the trouble of searching through a dictionary in the hope of finding a really long word. But, no matter how long the word written down by your friend you will always win the bet. Do you want to know how?

Well, there are actually two ways you can win. The first way is to write any four-letter word. Yes, that's right – any *four*-letter word. You then ask your friend what word she wrote down. When you are told you say, "Well, I have certainly written a longer word than you." Your friends will naturally want to see what you have written and they will laugh when you show them, for your word has only four letters!

They will all think that you

lost the bet. But then you explain, "I said I would write a longer word than you and that is what I have done – 'you' has only three letters, my word has four letters so I have written a longer word than 'you'."

The second way to win the bet (which you can show to people who have already seen you do the first version) is to write 'A longer word than you' on the paper. Once again you will certainly have won the bet!

MIND READING

While you are out of the room your friends place three objects on the table. These three objects can be anything they like. They then choose just one of the three items to concentrate on.

When you come into the room you immediately say which of the three objects is being thought of!

On this first occasion your friends may think that you picked the correct item purely by luck. But when you go on to do it several more times, and with different objects, they will be convinced that you can read minds.

Before reading how it is done just think about it for a moment. You do not know in advance what three objects will be placed on the table and not a word is spoken after you enter the room. There is no possible way you could know which object has been selected – and yet you guess correctly every time!

No, it is not done by witchcraft, or even by mind-reading. It is actually done by confederacy. One of your audience is your secret assistant. He or she signals to you which is the chosen object by a simple but subtle code.

If the object in the centre of the three is chosen your friend stands (or sits) with his feet together and pointing to the front (1). If the object to the right is chosen his right foot is pointed to the right (2). And if the left object is selected he points his left foot to the left (3). It is as simple as that!

Do not let the others in the room see you looking at your friend's feet or they may guess how the trick is done. A quick glance is enough to give you the information you need.

Because of the simplicity of this trick it is possible to perform it several times in succession, using different objects each time.

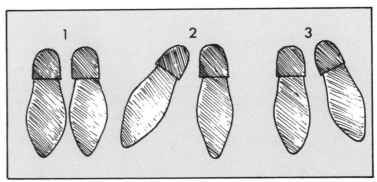

PERFECT SPIN

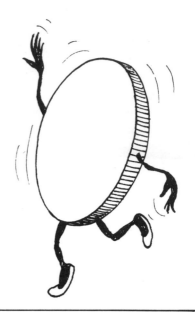

You show a coin on the palm of your outstretched hand. The coin is then tossed into the air where it spins rapidly.

When your friends try to do the same they find that they cannot make the coin spin as rapidly as you can.

The reason you can cause the coin to spin is that you secretly move your thumb inwards slightly as your hand moves upwards. As the coin leaves your palm the thumb hits the edge of the coin and causes it to spin. Immediately move your thumb away again and there will be no clue as to how you accomplished this intriguing feat.

Touch of Genius

YOU NEED:
- Five coins

Can you arrange the coins on a table in such a way that each coin touches all of the others?

No doubt you have already looked at the picture and discovered how this can be done. Your friends, however, may not find the problem so easy to solve.

STRAW OF STRENGTH

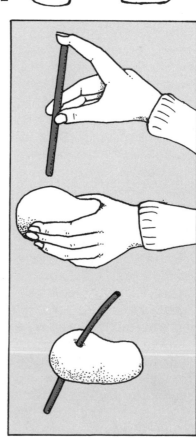

YOU NEED:
- A paper drinking straw
- A raw potato

You show your friends the straw and then push it into the potato.

That does not sound anything special, does it? But your friends will soon discover how special it is when they have a go, for their straws will simply buckle up when they are pushed into the potato.

What your friends do not realize is that there is a trick to this little stunt. All you have to do is hold your straw as shown in the illustration, with your finger over the top end of the straw. This traps a column of air inside the straw and makes it strong enough to penetrate the potato.

38

How To Move An Iceberg

YOU NEED:
- A glass of water
- An ice cube
- A piece of thin string
- Salt

Place an ice cube in a glass of water. Now give a friend the string and challenge him to lift the ice from the water using the piece of string. Your friend is not allowed to touch the ice cube.

Your friends may try all sorts of methods in order to

accomplish this feat, but there is only one way that works properly.

Lay the centre portion of the string across the top of the ice cube. Sprinkle some salt over the string and the top of the ice cube. (You forgot to tell your friends about the salt, didn't you!)

Wait a few seconds and then gently lift the string. The ice cube is now frozen to the string and can be lifted out of the glass quite easily.

TERCES EDOC

This puzzle has got rather a funny title. Can you work out what it is?

It is actually in code. There are lots of different codes you can use to write letters to your friends. Some codes are easy, some are quite difficult. This one is easy to make up, but it is clever enough to prevent your enemies from reading what you are writing about.

Here is a message using this code: TEEM EM TA THGINDIM THGINOT

Have you worked it out yet? If you look at it again you will see that the message is 'Meet me at midnight tonight'. All the words are written backwards.

Now you can use this method to write to your friends without anyone else knowing what you are writing about.

And the title? Secret Code, of course!

TOWER OF DRAUGHTS

YOU NEED:
- A set of draughts (or checkers)
- A table knife

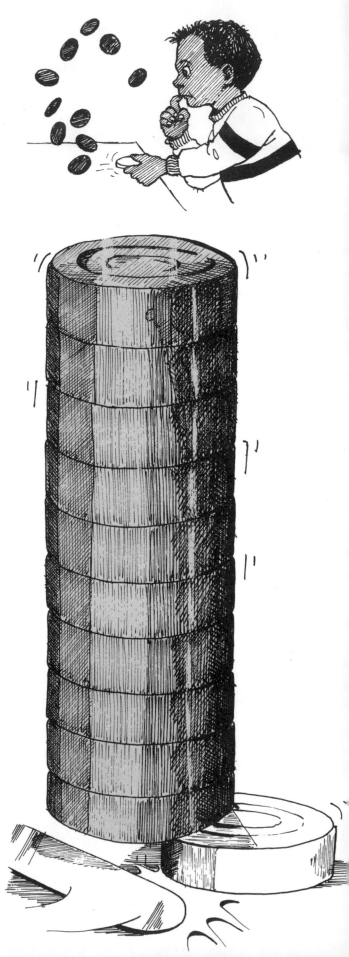

Put one white draught on a table with ten black draughts on top of it.

The problem you now put to someone is, "How can you remove the white piece from the bottom of the stack without touching the other pieces and without knocking over the whole tower?"

When your friend gives up you show how it is done. Take a table knife, place it flat on the table and hit the blade against the bottom draught to knock it out from under the black pieces.

A SECOND TOWER

Here is another draughts problem to puzzle your pals. In this version the white draught is positioned third or fourth from the bottom of a stack of black draughts. The problem is again to remove the white piece without the tower collapsing.

To do this you take one draught and stand it on edge alongside the tower. Place your forefinger on the top of the single draught and press downward and slightly backwards. The draught shoots forward, hits the tower and knocks out the white draught!

Before showing this to anyone, try it in private to practise the flicking movement and to discover which draught it will knock out.

40

COIN CROSS

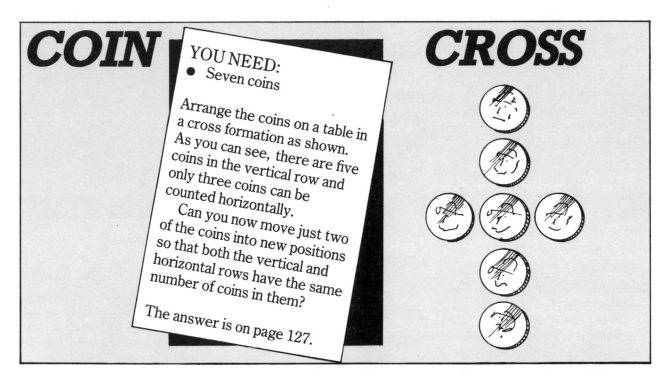

YOU NEED:
● Seven coins

Arrange the coins on a table in a cross formation as shown. As you can see, there are five coins in the vertical row and only three coins can be counted horizontally.

Can you now move just two of the coins into new positions so that both the vertical and horizontal rows have the same number of coins in them?

The answer is on page 127.

TURN THEM OVER

YOU NEED:
● Six coins

Place six coins in a row on the table. Arrange them so that the first three coins have their heads uppermost and the three coins to the right have their tails side showing, as in the picture (1).

What you now have to do is turn over two coins at a time until the coins alternate heads and tails along the row. The coins you turn over must be side by side and the row must end up in the order head, tail, head, tail, head, tail (2). There is just one more thing – you are allowed only three moves!

If you put this problem to your friends it is very likely that they will give up after a few tries, telling you that it is impossible.

You can then prove that it is not impossible by doing it. These are the three moves that you make:
Turn over coins 3 and 4.
Turn over coins 4 and 5.
Turn over coins 2 and 3.

That's all there is to it!

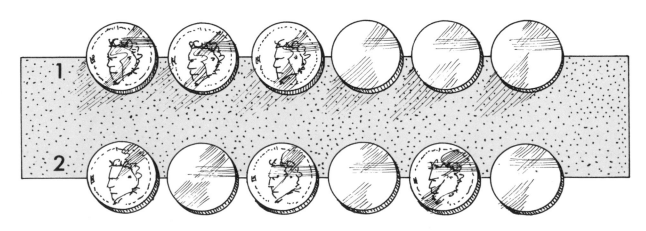

PICK IT UP

YOU NEED:
- A coin

Place the coin on the floor about 75 cm away from a wall. Tell a friend that he can have the coin if he can pick it up – subject to certain conditions.

The conditions are: your friend must stand with his heels touching the wall. In attempting to pick up the coin he is not allowed to move his heels away from the wall, neither can he lift them from the ground.

If these conditons are obeyed it will be impossible for your victim to pick up the coin. Try it out for yourself and see.

GLUED TO THE SPOT

In the position just described in 'Pick It Up' it is also impossible to jump even slightly off the floor, provided that your heels, hips and shoulders are touching the wall.

You can use this fact for a quite unusual bet. Tell a friend that you are able to make it impossible for her to jump off the floor. You will not hold her in any way and you will not weigh her down with anything heavy – but she will still not be able to jump.

When your friend accepts the challenge place her against the wall as described under 'Pick It Up' and ask her to try jumping, without bending or leaning forward in any way. Try as she may, she will not be able to do it and she will remain rooted firmly to the spot as if her shoes were glued to the floor.

YOU NEED:
- A glass of water
- A step-ladder or chair
- A broom handle

Hold a glass of water up against the ceiling. You will have to stand on a step-ladder or a chair to do this so be careful that you do not fall. Now place a broom handle against the base of the glass.

As you now have to get down from the chair you ask someone to hold the broom handle for a moment to keep the glass in position.

When you have got down you move the chair away – and leave your friend standing there! He dare not move because the glass will fall and he will get a soaking!

It is a rather naughty joke but an effective way to catch someone out!

Say to someone, "I bet I can sit somewhere where you cannot sit."

When your victim takes you up on this bet you go and sit on the sofa. As soon as you get up your friend will sit on the sofa. It looks as if you have lost the bet – but before you started you took the precaution of saying that you wanted three chances to accomplish the stunt – so you still have two attempts to go.

The second time around you sit on a chair. When you get up your victim will have no difficulty in sitting on the chair also. Only one attempt left!

On your last try you sit on your victim's lap. You have won the bet! Even the best contortionist in the world cannot sit on his own lap!

OFF AND ON

YOU NEED:
- A loose coat or jacket

This takes a bit of practice, but once you can do it smoothly you will find that it creates quite a laugh.

Lower your left arm until your jacket sleeve slides off the arm. The right arm now swings the coat around behind the body and then to the front. Keep the coat fairly low down as you do this so that when it comes to the front you can slip your left hand back into the top of the sleeve.

Now lift the coat up above your head, straighten your arms and the coat falls back down over your shoulders so you have it on once again.

With practice you should be able to do the complete action in one smooth sequence and it will impress people because it looks quite amazing.

Fill It Up

YOU NEED:
- Two liqueur glasses or small wine glasses
- A lot of sewing pins

For this amazing stunt you will need a great number of pins. It is very unlikely that you will be able to find enough pins at home so you will probably be better off buying some from your local store.

Fill one glass right to the top with water and fill the other glass to the top with pins. Now announce that you can put all the pins into the glass of water without spilling any of it – and wait for the jeers.

To accomplish this seemingly impossible feat is not at all difficult – surprising as that may seem. The secret is to transfer the pins to the glass of water one at a time.

If you are very careful all the pins will go into the water without it spilling over. Indeed you will probably find that you will need a number of pins in reserve for they will go into the water as well. In fact you will be very surprised yourself to see how many pins will go into a glass of water without the water spilling all over the place.

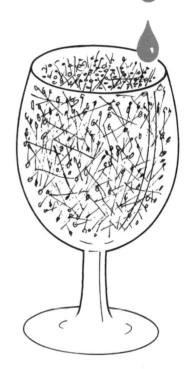
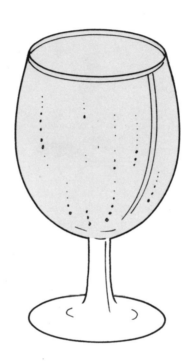

HOT AND COLD

YOU NEED:
- Three bowls

Fill the bowls with water as follows. The bowl to the left contains hot water, the one in the centre holds luke-warm water and the one to the right is full of cold water.

Put your left hand into the hot water and your right hand into the cold water. Leave your hands in the water for about a minute.

Now put both hands into the centre bowl. The water will feel cold to the left hand and yet at the same time actually hot to the right. It is quite a weird sensation to have both hands telling you different things at once!

Hair and Handkerchief

YOU NEED:
● A large handkerchief

Take the handkerchief and pull the centre up through your left fist. Provided that you did not pull too much of the material through your fist you will find that the handkerchief will stand up quite stiffly, as shown in the picture (1).

Now pretend to take a hair from your head. If there is someone bald watching you could pretend to take a hair from his head and say something like, "When I first started doing this trick he had a full head of hair."

Now pretend to tie one end of the hair around the uppermost point of the handkerchief. The right hand now pulls the invisible hair to the right and the handkerchief bends to the right (2) as if it is really attached to the hair. When the right hand moves back towards the handkerchief the material moves back to an upright position.

The movement of the handkerchief is really brought about by secretly lowering and then raising the left thumb. It is important that the movement of the handkerchief is timed to coincide with the movements of the right hand, so as to give your audience the impression that there really is a hair.

'Pull' the hair to the right once again and then bend forward and pretend to bite the hair with your teeth. At the same time move your left thumb up so that the handkerchief moves to an upright position once again.

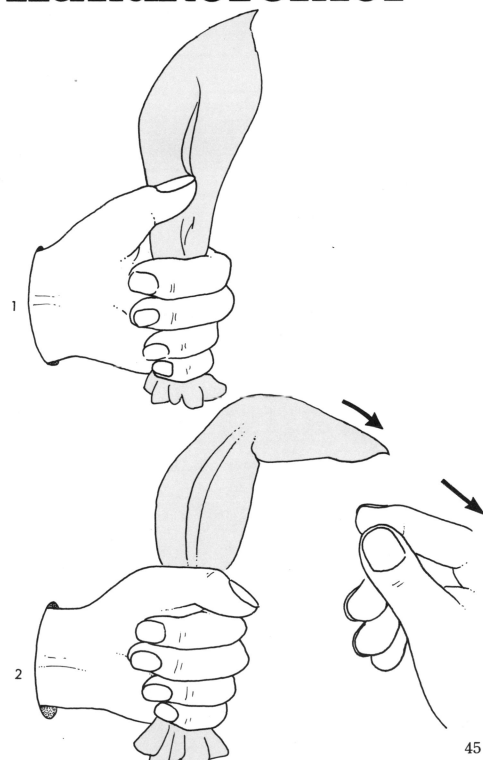

1

2

WATER WIZARDRY

YOU NEED:
● A tumbler
● A comb

Place the empty tumbler in the sink and then turn a tap on slowly. The water from the tap should just miss the glass.

How can you now make the water go into the glass without anything touching either the water or the glass?

Quite amazingly, the only thing you need is a comb! Run the comb through your hair a few times. This charges the comb with static electricity. Now hold the comb near to the running water and, believe it or not, the water will bend towards the comb so that you can direct it into the glass.

Do not touch the water with the comb or this trick will not work.

TOPSY TURVY WATER

YOU NEED:
● A glass of water

Just imagine everyone's gasp of horror when you take a glass of water and then start waving your arm over your head!

Hold the glass of water in your hand. Your arm is outstretched and the elbow is underneath the arm. Now swing your arm over your head in an anticlockwise direction, as shown by the dotted lines in the picture.

You should finish up with your arm stretched out to the side once again but this time the elbow will be pointing upwards. And you never spilled a drop!

For obvious reasons you should practise this stunt out in the garden until you are sure you can do it without drenching everything and everybody in sight!

46

How To See Through Your Hand

YOU NEED:

- A magazine or sheet of newspaper

Did you know there is a hole in your hand? Of course you didn't because there isn't! But it will seem as if there is when you try this amazing trick.

Roll the magazine or sheet of newspaper into a tube. You can use sticky tape to hold the tube together if you wish but it is not absolutely necessary.

Hold the tube up to your right eye so you can see through it. Now hold your left hand up in front of your left eye but keep your eye open. Look through both eyes at the same time and it will seem as if there is a large hole you can look through in the palm of your left hand.

THE DEAD FINGER

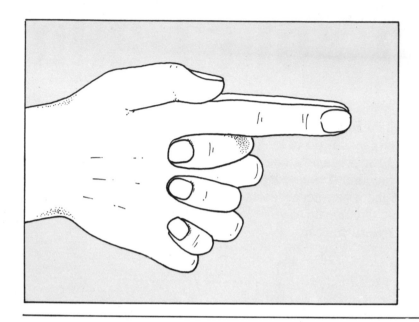

With your right hand clasp someone's left hand. You both have your forefingers extended as shown in the picture.

Now ask your friend to use the finger and thumb of her other hand to feel the forefingers. As she moves her hand up and down (her thumb touching her own finger and her forefinger touching yours) she will receive a strange sensation of numbness – as if she has lost some feeling in her finger.

I'M NO PUSH OVER

Show everyone a sheet of newspaper and say, "I am so strong that I can stand on this newspaper in such a way that no one will be able to push me off."

Sooner or later someone will offer to take up your challenge – but there are a few rules they must observe.

You are allowed to put the paper on the floor wherever you wish. Only one person at a time may take up the challenge. He or she is to try to push or pull you off the paper using only their own strength. Your challenger is not allowed to get anyone else to help, neither may he or she use any object to help push or pull you off the paper.

When the terms are agreed you are ready to spring your trap. You open the door to the room and place the paper down so that it is half in one room and half in the other. You get your opponent to stand on one half of the paper. Then you shut the door and stand on the other half of the paper. With the door shut firmly between you there is no way that your opponent can even touch you, let alone force you off the paper!

STRING THROUGH THE NECK

YOU NEED:
- A piece of string about 75 cm long

1. Tie the string into a loop, and place it around your neck. Put your thumbs into the loop at each end in front of your body. Allow everyone to get a good look at this position as you explain that you are going to pass the string through your neck by magic.
Turn your back and get someone to examine the back of your neck. This is just to make sure that your head is not detachable or that you do not have a secret slot in your neck!
2. While the back of your neck is being examined, secretly slip the forefinger of your left hand into the loop of string which you have been holding with your right thumb.
3. Now turn round to face your audience once again. At the same time allow your left thumb to slip from its loop and move the left hand to the left.
4. This action will pull the loop of string around your neck. By the time you are back facing your audience the string will have completed its journey and is now held in front of the body between the right thumb and the left forefinger.
To everyone watching it seems that the string has travelled right through your neck.

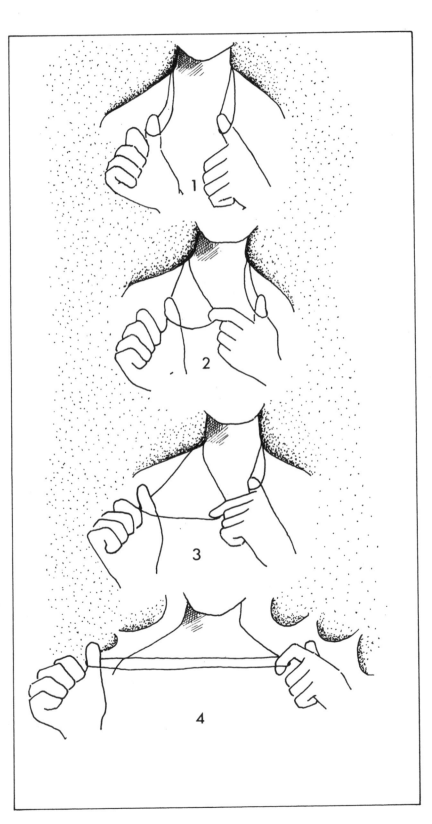

HOW TO FOLD A TRIANGLE

YOU NEED:

● A square sheet of paper

Can you take a square sheet of paper and fold it into the shape of an equilateral triangle? The triangle must be as large as you can possibly make it and you are not allowed to use a pencil, a ruler, or scissors in its construction.

Sounds difficult, doesn't it. And it is! But only if you do not know the answer. Because of this it is a good puzzle to baffle your friends for they will not be able to do it – but you can.

All you have to do is follow the instructions. You will find these easier to understand if you go through them with a square sheet of paper in your hands and try it move by move.

1. We will identify the four corners of the paper as A, B, C and D. First fold the side BD on to AC. Open out the paper and you will have a crease down the centre. We will call this crease EF.

2. Fold corner D up to touch the line EF. The fold you make should go through the middle of corner C.

3. Fold corner B down on top of DG.

4. Open up corner B and there will be a crease across the top right corner of the paper. We will call this crease HG. Now fold the edge CD until it touches the crease CG. We will call this crease CI.

5. Open out the paper and the creases should look like this.

6. Now fold the paper between the points H and I. Do the same between the points C and H. The equilateral triangle CHI should now be clearly marked on the paper.

Aren't you clever!

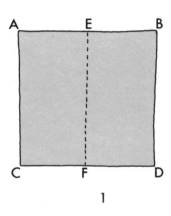

1

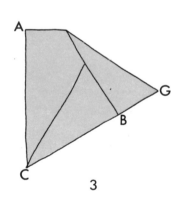

2

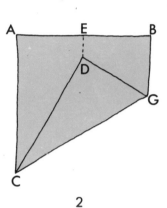

3

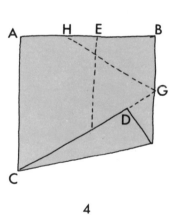

4

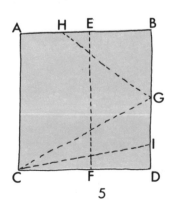

5

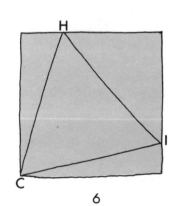

6

LINKING PAPER CLIPS

YOU NEED:
- A piece of paper about 5 cm by 15 cm
- Two paper clips

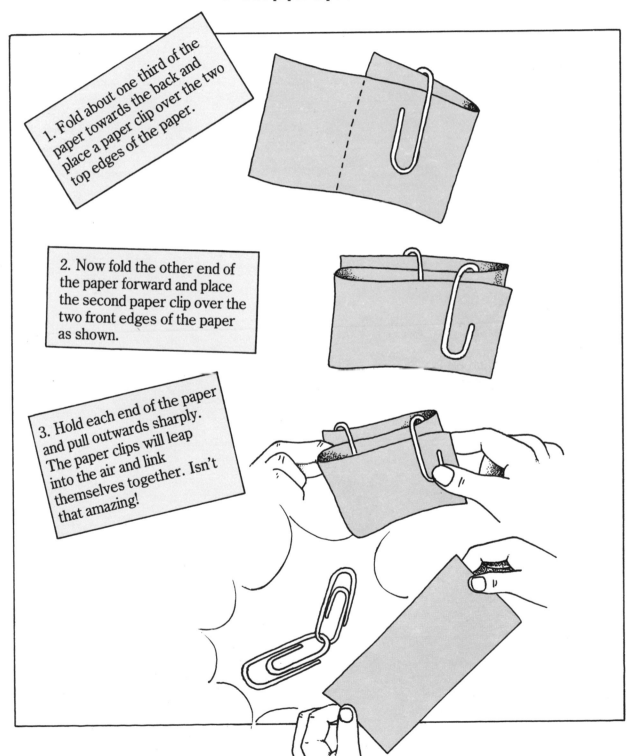

1. Fold about one third of the paper towards the back and place a paper clip over the two top edges of the paper.

2. Now fold the other end of the paper forward and place the second paper clip over the two front edges of the paper as shown.

3. Hold each end of the paper and pull outwards sharply. The paper clips will leap into the air and link themselves together. Isn't that amazing!

A NOISE MAKER

YOU NEED:

- A piece of paper about 5 cm by 10 cm
- Scissors

You probably do not need any advice on how to make a noise. But if you would like to make an interesting new noise that is different to the one you normally make, then you can try this.

1. Fold the paper in half.
2. Now cut out two small triangles from the folded edge.
3. Each half of the paper is now folded in half again so that the centre section stands up from the rest.
4. Hold the paper between your first and second fingers, bring it up to your mouth and blow. You will produce a screeching noise that will make all your friends jump out of their skin!

THE FLYING CROSS

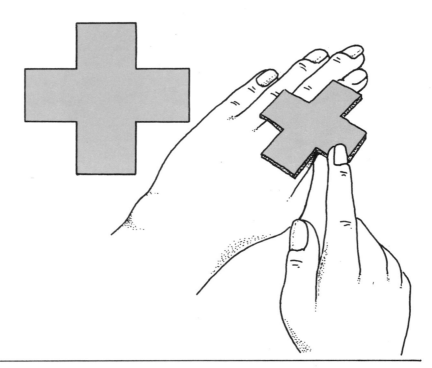

YOU NEED:
- A sheet of thin card

Cut out the shape of a cross from the card, as shown.

Place the cross on the back of your left hand with one of its arms lying along the length of your forefinger. Tuck your left thumb out of the way. Now, using your right forefinger, hit the edge of the cross that overlaps your hand and the cross will fly away. With practice you will be able to hit it so that it spins back to you, rather like a boomerang.

BRIDGE OF KNIVES

YOU NEED:
- Four glasses
- Three long-bladed table knives

Place three glasses on the table along with the knives. Now show everyone a fourth glass and challenge them to build a bridge connecting the three glasses, that is strong enough to support the fourth glass. Only the three knives can be used, with the handles resting on the glasses and the blades touching at the centre.

The secret of accomplishing this task lies in the way the knife blades are interlocked at the centre and it is very unlikely that your friends will work out how to do it.

Look at the illustration and you will see how it is done. The first knife goes over the blade of the second knife and under the third. The second knife goes over the third and under the first. And the third knife goes over the first and beneath the second.

Balance the whole lot on the rims of the three glasses and the fourth glass can then be placed in the centre of the knives without fear of your bridge collapsing.

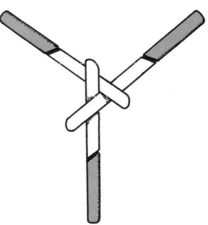

THE READY-SLICED BANANA

YOU NEED:
- A banana (a ripe one is best)
- A needle and thread

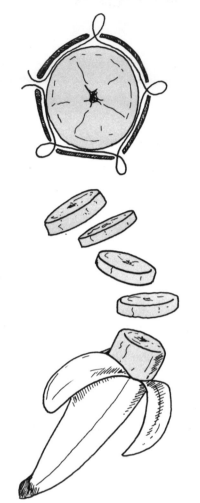

We live in an age of some fantastic labour-saving devices. But have you ever come across a self-slicing banana? It sounds like the height of laziness. There is of course no such thing (yet!) but you can give your friends the impression that there is by using a little trickery.

Push the needle into a corner of the banana (in case you haven't noticed, bananas are not perfectly round but actually have five sides). Push the needle under the skin and out at the next corner. Pull most of the thread through but make sure that you leave the end of the thread sticking out from the first hole.

Now push the needle back into the second hole and across, under the skin, to the next corner. Keep working like this from corner to corner until you come back to the original hole. The illustration shows a cross-section of the banana at this point.

Take both ends of the thread at the same time and pull the thread out of the first hole. This action slices the fruit inside the skin.

Do exactly the same again a little further along the banana. Repeat this several times down the whole length of the banana.

The banana looks quite ordinary – and no one is going to look at it closely anyway. But when you peel it later in the day (with some of your friends present, of course) the banana will emerge from its skin ready sliced. Isn't modern technology wonderful!

TOUCH IT

Hold up your right arm. Now bend your right hand down as far as you can – as if you are trying to touch your right elbow. As you are doing this ask someone watching if he can touch his elbow with his hand.

Hopefully, your friend will actually try to do this. But eventually he will have to say, "No."

You then say, "I can." And then you touch your right elbow with your left hand!

UNTOUCHABLE

Can you put your left hand somewhere where your right hand cannot touch it?

Place your left hand on your right elbow – the right hand cannot touch it there.

FINGER SHOCK

Bite the tips of your little fingers for about half a minute. Now link your little fingers together as shown and pull. You should be able to feel something like a mild electric shock in your fingers. Strange, isn't it!

Get It Across

Place any object, a coin, a pencil, a ball (it doesn't matter what) on your right hand.

Now stretch your arms straight out to the sides as the person is doing in the picture.

Keeping your arms outstretched can you get the object over on to your left hand? You must not bring the hands together, bend your elbows, or even bend your wrists to do this.

As has been said before in this book – the solution to this problem is really quite simple. But please try to solve it before going on to read the answer. If you have had a go and are unable to find the answer then you can read on.

This is what you have to do. Keeping your arms straight, turn your body until you can place the object you are holding on your right hand on to a table. Now turn a bit more until your left hand comes near to the table-top and you can pick up the object quite easily.

Now that you know the answer, challenge your friends to try it out for themselves and see if they can solve the problem.

HANDS UP

Stand in a doorway (you will find this a lot easier to do if the door is open!).

Hold your hands down at your sides and then press the backs of your hands against the sides of the door frame. Press your hands against the frame as hard as you can for at least a minute.

Now step away from the door and your arms will feel as if they are floating upwards.

Strange, isn't it!

DO IT YOURSELF

Puzzles like the ones on this page are very simple to devise so you can make up some of your own quite easily. All you have to do is draw a shape and then cut it up. It is as simple as that!

Put each set of pieces in an envelope and write the name of the shape that has to be formed on the outside of the envelope.

Leave them for a while until you have forgotten exactly

how you made them and you will have some fun puzzling them out yourself. In fact it might take you some time.

Some ideas are given in the pictures – but try to make up some of your own as well.

YOU NEED:
- A square piece of thin card and a pencil
- Scissors

Copy this diagram on to the card and then cut along all the lines to make nine pieces of different shapes and sizes.

Hand all nine pieces to a friend (who will be getting rather fed up with all these puzzles by now!) and see if he or she can arrange them into the shape of a square.

MAKE IT SQUARE

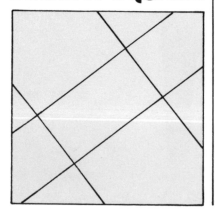

FOUR
SQUARE PUZZLE

YOU NEED:
- A square piece of thin card and a pencil
- Scissors

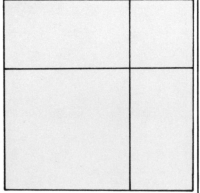

Copy this drawing on to the card and then cut it into four along the lines shown.

Hand the four pieces to a friend with the challenge to arrange them into a square.

YOU NEED:
- A square piece of thin card and a pencil
- Scissors

Copy this design on to the sheet of card and then cut it along the lines so that you have four triangles.

Hand the triangles to a friend and ask him or her to arrange the pieces into the shape of a square. Believe it or not, it is quite difficult to do this!

SQUARE THE △'S

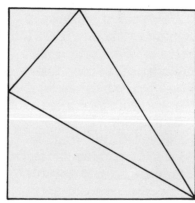

IMPOSSIBLE LIFT

Place your hand, palm down, flat on a table. Now bend the second finger inwards so that the back of the joint is touching the table. Keep all your other fingers firmly on the table and see if you can lift your thumb from the table-top.

Easy wasn't it? But that is not the problem. Replace your thumb on the table and try to

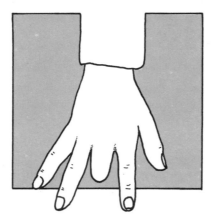

lift your little finger and put it back down again. You should have found that was easy to do also. So, let's try something else.

With the rest of your fingers in contact with the table try lifting your third finger. This you will find very difficult indeed – for it just cannot be done! Now try the same stunt on your friends.

EGG BALANCE

YOU NEED:
- Two eggs
- Salt

You show an egg and try to stand it on its end on a table. Naturally it rolls over. Then you take another egg, say some magic words, and place it on the table. This one stands upright! But when you hand the same egg to someone else to have a go they will find that it just cannot be done.

Before showing this trick you prepared the egg in a rather clever way. All you have to do is to dampen the base of the egg and then dip it into some salt. Blow all the loose salt crystals away. Some of the salt will remain sticking to the egg and this will be enough to hold it upright on the table. (Be careful not to let anyone else look at the egg too closely.)

As you hand the egg to someone else you casually wipe your hand over the eggshell and remove the salt.

57

Weight-Lifting Radish

YOU NEED:
- A radish
- A plate

Did you know that the humble radish is capable of lifting a heavy weight? Well it is, and this is how you do it.

Take a large, firm and juicy radish. It is important that it should still have part of its stalk in place as you will need this to hold on to later.

Cut the top half off the radish and scoop out a little of the inside to make a small depression. Be careful that you do not damage the cut edge of the radish when you do this.

Now press the radish on to the centre of a clean plate. Lift the radish by its stalk and, with a bit of luck, the plate will be lifted as well.

It is a good idea to do this over a soft surface – just in case it does not work.

STICKY FORK

YOU NEED:
- An ordinary dinner fork

You show the fork and then clasp your hands together. The fork appears to stick to your hands like magic. Your friends may think that there is some glue on the fork but when you hand it to someone else to have a go everyone will then realize that the fork is perfectly ordinary.

Although the people watching think they can see all your fingers when the hands are clasped together, the middle finger of the right hand is actually out of sight behind all the others. It is the hidden finger that actually supports the fork.

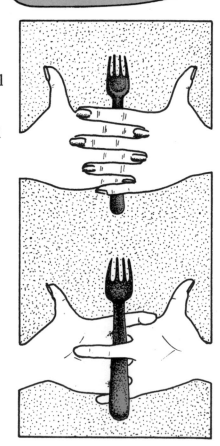

A MAGIC EGG

YOU NEED:
- An egg
- A pin
- Fine dry sand
- Tissue paper
- Glue

This stunt takes a little bit of preparation but it is well worth the effort. Take an ordinary chicken's egg and make a hole in each end of it with a pin. You will have to push the pin through the shell several times at each end to make the holes big enough.

Blow through one of the holes and the contents will be forced out through the other hole. Make sure you have a saucer handy to catch the contents as they come out of the shell. (Keep the contents in the fridge for baking or scrambled egg later.)

Wash out the inside of the shell by placing it under warm running water. Handle the egg very carefully for the shell is quite fragile.

When the eggshell is completely dry pour some fine dry sand into it (1). A heaped teaspoonful is about enough.

Seal the holes in the shell with glue and tissue paper. The tissue paper should be of a similar colour to the eggshell so it will not be seen (or it can be painted the same colour).

This special egg can be used to perform some remarkable balancing feats (2). Because the sand always runs to the bottom of the egg it will remain balanced in whatever position you place it.

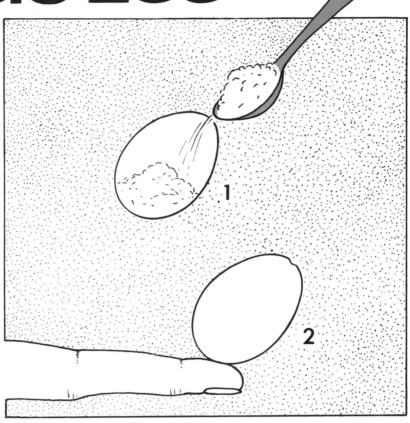

FLOATING SALT CELLAR

YOU NEED:
- A salt cellar
- A toothpick

At the dinner table you place the tip of your finger on the top of the salt cellar – and the cellar sticks to your finger by magic.

What your audience do not see is the fact that you have secretly pushed a toothpick into the top of the cellar. By holding the toothpick between finger and thumb as shown it looks as if the cellar is stuck to your fingertip.

After showing this trick it is fairly easy to pull the toothpick out and drop it on your lap without being seen. No one will ever guess your secret.

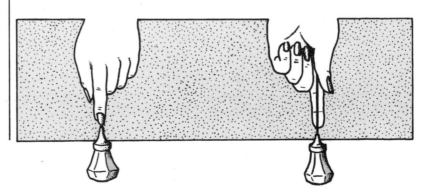

THE DANCING WIRE

YOU NEED:
- Two fine glasses
- A piece of wire

The wire must be long enough to rest across the mouth of one of the glasses, plus a little bit extra to bend over the rim of the glass.

Half fill both of the glasses with water. Dip your finger into the water and run it around the rim of one of the glasses. With practice you will be able to produce a weird whistling noise.

By adjusting the amount of water in the glass you can change the pitch of the noise you create. Keep adjusting the water level in one of the glasses until both glasses produce exactly the same note when you rub the rim.

Place the wire on the top of one of the glasses and then rub the rim of the other to produce the noise. If the two glasses have been tuned properly the wire will start to dance! The glasses should be fairly close together for this stunt to work correctly.

Bridge of Paper

YOU NEED:
- A sheet of paper
- Three glasses

Place two glasses on a table, mouth up. Across the top of the glasses lay a piece of paper (1).

Now ask someone if they can balance a third glass on the paper and leave it there with no other form of support.

The paper will not, of course, support the glass as it is. But it will if you make a number of pleats along the length of the paper to give it extra strength. (2).

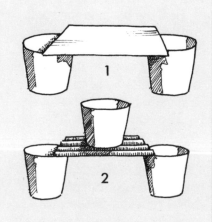

A DRINK FOR A GHOST

YOU NEED:
- A glass
- Sticky tape
- A drinking straw

Pour some water (or lemonade if you prefer) into a glass. Now stick strips of sticky tape across the top of the glass in a criss-cross formation. Cover as much of the mouth of the glass as you can, but make sure that there are at least a few gaps.

Tell everyone that your house is haunted (this trick has to be done at night-time) and that the ghost enjoys a drink.

Ask for the lights to be put out for a short while. When you ask for the lights to be switched on again most of the liquid has gone! The ghost obviously enjoyed his drink!

The tape makes it look impossible for you to have drunk the liquid – but of course you did. As soon as the room is in darkness you remove a drinking straw from your pocket and push it through one of the gaps in the tape. Drink as much as you can before asking for the lights to be put back on.

If, by any chance, you push the straw in and discover that the liquid has gone then maybe there really is a ghost in the house!

A CRAFTY DRINK

YOU NEED:
- A glass of water
- A hat

Place the glass of water on a table and then cover it with the hat (or a box). You tell everyone that you are going to drink the water without lifting the hat. You then make some sucking noises as if you were drinking the water. Tell your friends that you have finished.

Sooner or later one of the people watching will get curious and lift the hat to see if the water is still there. As soon as the hat is lifted you pick up the glass and drink the water.

You have now done what you said you would do. You have drunk the water without lifting the hat. You didn't lift the hat, someone else did!

FIND THE LADY

1

YOU NEED:
- Five old playing cards
- A paper clip
- Glue

Glue the five cards together, with a Queen as the centre card (1).

You show these cards to your audience and point out the position of the Queen. Then you hand someone a paper clip, turn the cards face down, and ask that the clip be placed on the Queen. Your friend naturally puts the clip on the centre card (2). But when the cards are turned over the clip is nowhere near the Queen, it is on the end card (3)! This trick works by itself – try it and see.

2

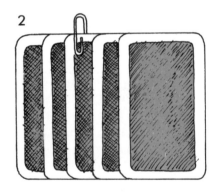

3

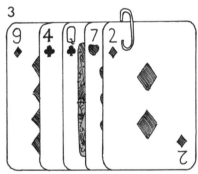

HIDE THE PIPS ♠♦♣♥

YOU NEED:
- A pack of playing cards

Take the four Fives from a pack of cards. Can you now arrange the cards so that only four pips are visible on each card?

It is easy to hide one pip on the first three cards but the fourth may prove a little more difficult. How do you do it?

By now you will have looked at the picture on this page and will have realized the arrangement that is necessary to hide the pips. But your friends, who do not know the answer, may find it a little more difficult.

When putting this problem to your friends tell them to ignore the small pips below the numbers on the corners of the cards, for sooner or later some clever person is going to mention them if you don't.

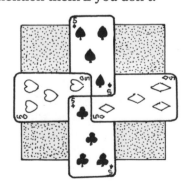

● A pack of cards

6 CARD INTERLOCK

Spread six playing cards on the table and challenge anyone to pick up five of the cards by lifting only the sixth, without just piling them on top of each other.

It is a trick that will cause your friends some problems. But you will not have any trouble doing it because you have tried it out in private first.

All you have to do is position the cards on the table in the order shown by the numbers in the picture. Now tuck the centre portion of card 5 under card 1 and do the same with card 6.

By lifting card 2 between your finger and thumb all the other cards can be lifted at the same time.

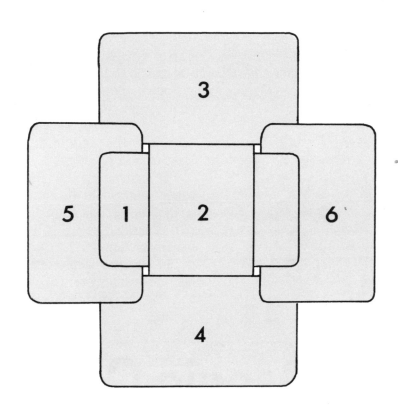

11 CARD INTERLOCK

When you have shown how clever you are with the 'Six Card Interlock', unlink the cards and spread them on the table again.

Add another five cards with the challenge to lift ten of the cards with the eleventh.

To do this you have to interlock the first six cards as already described. You then place the seventh card on card 2. The remaining four are positioned as before, with the last two tucked under card 1.

All eleven cards are now interlocked together so that by supporting the middle card all the other cards will be lifted as well.

Use an old pack as the cards will be less slippery.

NUMBER MAGIC

YOU NEED:
- Paper and a pencil

Take a sheet of paper and write down, in large numbers, the following sum:

462
307
299
101
134
———
1303

Hand the paper to a friend with a challenge to change the sum to three numbers which still add up to 1303.

Your friend must not write on the paper nor rub anything out. And she is not allowed to cut or tear the paper in any way. Quite a problem!

The answer is to fold the paper as shown in the picture so that the second number (307) falls half-way over the fourth number (101).

The sum now consists of only three numbers: 462, 707 and 134, and yet it still adds up to 1303.

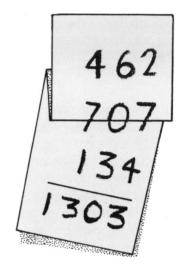

462
707
134
———
1303

The Magic Circle

YOU NEED:
- Paper and a pencil

Draw a circle on a piece of paper and then turn your back. While your back is turned you ask someone to write any number from 1 to 9 in the circle.

Then ask the same person to write the same number to the right and the left of the magic circle. Then to write the number 3 both above and below the circle.

He must now add up all the figures and tell you the total. As soon as he does so you can pretend to read his mind and tell everyone which number is in the centre of the magic circle.

To do this all you have to do is divide the spectator's total by 3 and then subtract 2.

Here is an example. If the chosen number is 8 the total of all the numbers (as shown in the picture) will be 30. So $30 \div 3 = 10$. And $10 - 2 = 8$, the chosen number!

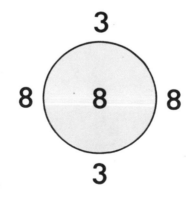

3

8   8   8

3

THE MAGIC MULTIPLE

YOU NEED:
- A calculator

If you have a calculator you can show your friends the remarkable way that the number 15873 reacts when multipled by a multiple of 7. These are the results you will get:

$15873 \times 7 = 111111$
$15873 \times 14 = 222222$
$15873 \times 21 = 333333$
$15873 \times 28 = 444444$
$15873 \times 35 = 555555$
$15873 \times 42 = 666666$
$15873 \times 49 = 777777$
$15873 \times 56 = 888888$
$15873 \times 63 = 999999$

Try continuing the multiple sequence to see what happens.

The Vanishing Number

YOU NEED:
● Paper and a pencil

Announce that you are going to show the amazing vanishing number trick. You say that you can make any number vanish and ask someone to call out any number between one and nine.

You now say that you are going to write down several numbers including the chosen number. When you say the magic word the chosen number will disappear but all the other numbers will remain.

It sounds impossible, doesn't it? But it can be done – and this is how. Before you write all the numbers on the paper you fold the bottom corner of the paper up. Now write down a row of numbers that includes the chosen number – but the chosen number is written on the folded up corner as shown.

You show the row of numbers and then make the chosen number vanish by simply straightening out the piece of paper!

91652 7 438

YOU NEED:
● Paper and a pencil

Ask someone to write down any six-figure number. Next, she is to add the digits of her number together. The total she gets is then placed under the first number and is subtracted from it.

She is now asked to ring round any of the digits contained in the answer – then add all the unringed numbers in the answer together.

When she gives you the total of the digits in the answer (leaving out the ringed number) you can immediately tell her what number she circled. At no time have you seen any of her calculations and you had no idea what number she chose to start with, so how did you know what number she ringed?

All you have to do is subtract her given number from the next highest multiple of 9. So, if her answer was 13, the next multiple of 9 is 18 and the ringed number will be 5 (18 − 13). If the answer was 24, the ringed number is 3 (27 − 24).

Here is a complete example.
Write down any six digit number: 294735
Add the digits together:

$$(2+9+4+7+3+5=30)$$

Subtract the answer from the chosen number:

```
294735
    30
294705
```

Ring round any number in the answer:

294⑦05

Add the remaining numbers together:

$$(2+9+4+0+5=20).$$

You are told that the answer is 20.
The next multiple of 9 is 27.
Subtract 20 from 27 and you get 7, which is the number that was ringed.

65

FIGURE IT OUT

YOU NEED:
- Paper and pencil
- A box
- A blindfold

Here is a simple mind-reading trick to baffle your friends.

Take a sheet of paper and write the numbers 1 to 9 on it as shown in the drawing. Then tear the paper up into nine squares and drop all of the pieces into a box.

Get someone to blindfold you and then ask them to hand you any one of the pieces of paper. Ask them to concentrate on whether the number on the paper is odd or even and you will read their mind.

You will be right every time

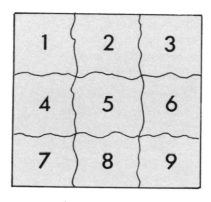

because all you have to do is feel the edges of the paper. If you look at the drawing you will see that all the even numbers will have one straight edge, while the odd numbers all have two straight edges. The only exception is number 5, which has no straight edges.

As soon as you are handed a piece of paper secretly feel for the straight edges. One straight edge means it is an even number and two straight edges mean that it is an odd number. If you are handed the piece with no straight edges you can tell everyone that you think it is an odd number – and then baffle them even further by announcing that the number you are holding is 5!

THOUGHT TRANSFERENCE

While you are out of the room your friends choose any object in the room. When you return one of your friends points to various objects. After a while you say, "That's it!" Much to everyone's surprise your friend is pointing to the object that everyone chose.

To do this mind-reading trick you arrange a simple code with your friend beforehand. Just before pointing to the object that has been chosen she must point at something that is red.

When you are performing the trick, she points to objects and as soon as she points to something that is red you know that the next item will be the one chosen.

If you want to perform this trick several times it is a good idea to arrange a sequence of colours with your secret assistant. So, the first time the object before the chosen one is red. Next time you do the trick you use blue, then yellow, green, and so on. This will make it much more difficult for anyone else in the room to work out how the trick is done.

IMMOBILE MONEY

YOU NEED:
- A playing card
- A coin

Balance a playing card on the tip of your left forefinger.

Now place a coin on the centre of the card, directly above your fingertip.

If you now use your right hand to hit the right corner of the card it will fly away, leaving the coin balanced on the tip of your finger.

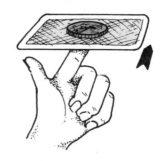

MORE MIND-READING

In many ways this trick is like 'Thought Transference'. But this time the mind-reader can have his back turned. He can even be out of the room but he can still say which object has been chosen.

Any object is selected by the people in the room while you are somewhere else. When you return your friend (and secret assistant) points to objects in turn and says each time, "Is it this?" You know instantly when the selected object is reached.

Once again there is a code used by yourself and your secret assistant. This time it is a number code. You first agree on a number, something like 5947. On the first performance of the trick the fifth item he points to is the chosen one, next time it is the ninth one, and so on. It is as simple as that.

This code is so simple that you can even do your mind-reading over the telephone – you do not even have to be in the same house and yet you can identify the object selected by the audience!

Balancing Coin

YOU NEED:
- A coin
- A pin

Your friends will be amazed when you take a coin and balance it upright on your outstretched fingers. They will think that you are a talented juggler.

Whatever you do, make sure that you do not tell them that the coin is really supported by a hidden pin held between your fingers. Let them think that your skill is the result of many years of hard practice.

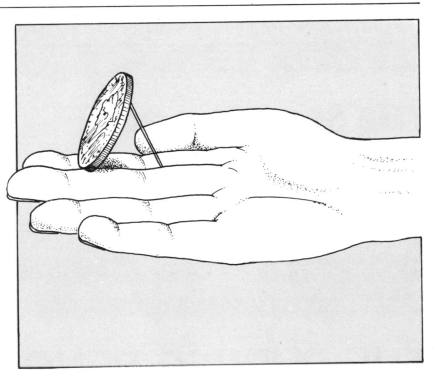

COINS
AT THE
FINGERTIPS

YOU NEED:
- Four coins

Place a coin on the tip of each of the fingers of one hand.

Now try to get all the coins, balanced on top of each other, on the tip of your first finger.

You must not use your thumb to help you do this and you are certainly not allowed to use your other hand.

No, there is no trick to it this time. This is just a test of your balancing and juggling skills. Get all your friends trying it as well. It makes quite a good game.

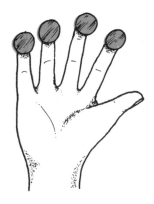

JUGGLING WITH MONEY

YOU NEED:
- Four or five coins

This takes a little bit of practice, but it is not very difficult to do.

Bend your elbow so that your hand comes up to your shoulder. Now balance four or five coins on your elbow.

Now drop your arm forward and down quickly and try to catch the coins as they fall.

The art in doing this is to keep your elbow bent slightly throughout the action. Turn your palm towards the floor and catch the coins, with a slight flick of the wrist, at the point marked X in the picture.

Once you get the hang of this stunt it is really quite easy to do – but it looks extremely impressive.

Try it with only one coin to start with – it saves having to pick up lots of coins from the floor if you fail!

THE SPINNING COIN

YOU NEED:
- Two pins
- A coin with a milled edge

Place the coin flat on a table and then pick it up with the two pins. The points of the pins are pressed against each side of the coin, as shown.

Keeping a tight grip of the

coin with the pins and making sure that your hands are steady bring the coin up to your face.

Now blow on the coin and it will spin round very fast. You will find that you do not have to blow very hard to do this and that a gentle, continuous blow gives best results. You may need some practice to find the right angle, however.

THE RUBBER PENCIL

YOU NEED:
- A long pencil

Hold the pencil between your finger and thumb at about one third of the distance from one end.

Now move your hand up and down, at the same time allowing the pencil to rock to and fro between your fingers. You don't need to rock it very fast.

To the people watching it will appear that the pencil is made of rubber. Practise in front of the mirror first to see what effect you get.

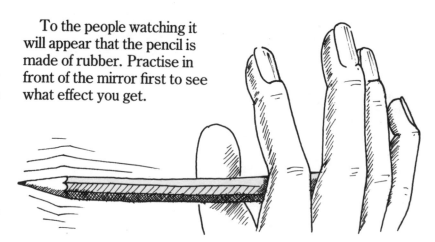

The Magic Pencil Box

YOU NEED:
- A pencil
- A matchbox

If you want to show someone 'The Rubber Pencil' why not produce the pencil by magic from a box that is far too small to hold it? Impossible? Not if you know the secret.

All you need is an ordinary matchbox. Or, at least, your friends will think it is ordinary. What you do not tell them is that you have secretly cut

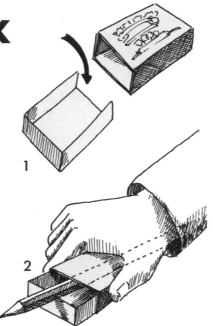

away one end of the drawer especially for this trick.

Put the drawer back in the box and then push the pencil into the open end of the box as far as it will go. The other end of the pencil is hidden up your sleeve.

You are now ready to show the trick. All you have to do is open the drawer of the matchbox and pull out the pencil!

Put the matchbox away in your pocket and tell everyone that the pencil is made of rubber (which it isn't) and that it was folded up inside the matchbox. This gives you a good excuse to amaze everyone even more with 'The Rubber Pencil' trick.

THE FLYING PENCIL

YOU NEED:
- A long pencil
- An elastic band

Place the elastic band over your first finger. Now take the pencil and push it down on to the lower part of the elastic band as shown in the picture.

Place your thumb against the pencil to hold it in position. When you remove your thumb the pencil will shoot up into the air.

FINGER FUN

YOU NEED:
- A sheet of paper

Make a very small hole in the centre of a sheet of paper. Show this to your friends and challenge anyone to push their finger through the centre of the paper without tearing it.

As you have made the hole very small no one's finger will go through it and they will all have to give up.

You then pick up the paper, roll it into a tube and push your finger down the centre of the tube!

PUSH IT THROUGH

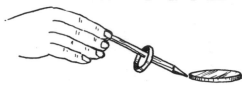

YOU NEED:
- A ring
- A coin
- A pencil

Show a finger ring and a large coin. The coin must be bigger than the ring. Press the coin against the ring as you say to a friend "Do you think you could push this coin through the ring?" Hand the ring to your friend to have a go.

Your friend will not be able to do it, of course. But you then do it in rather a cheeky way.

Place the coin on a table and hold the ring near it. Now take a pencil from your pocket, push it through the ring to touch the coin. Use the pencil to push the coin along the table and you have done what you said. You are pushing the coin through the ring!

STAR MATCHES

YOU NEED:
- Five used matches
- A plate

Bend the matches in half, being careful not to break them completely in two. Now arrange them on a plate in the shape of a ten-pointed star, as shown (1).

The problem you now present to your friends is, "How can you change the ten-pointed star into a five-pointed star without touching any of the matches and without touching the plate?"

The solution to this problem is quite magical. All you have to do is allow a few drops of water (from a sponge) to fall on the centre of the star. The matches will now move by themselves into the new formation (2)!

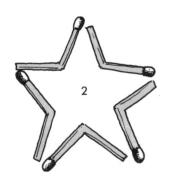

A Rattling Good Trick

YOU NEED:
- Three empty matchboxes
- One matchbox with matches
- A strip of bandage or tape

You show three matchboxes; when you shake them two are empty and the third contains some matches. When you mix the boxes up on the table your spectators will never be able to find the full box, no matter how hard they watch your movements.

You can repeat this trick several times, but your friends will never pick the right box – unless you want them to. The spectators never succeed because all three matchboxes are empty.

What your audience do not notice is that you shake the empty boxes with your left hand and the apparently full box with your right hand. You do this because attached to your right wrist by a strip of bandage and hidden by your sleeve is the fourth box containing the matches.

You can make any of the three boxes on the table appear to contain matches simply by picking it up and shaking it with the right hand.

Your audience will be completely taken in by this. No one will realize that the sound is not coming from the box you are holding, but from the one you have cleverly hidden up your sleeve.

THE FARMER'S PROBLEM

YOU NEED:
- 13 matches

A farmer had six sheep and 13 pieces of fencing. Using the fencing he built six pens, all the same size, so each animal could be kept in a separate pen.

Arrange the 13 matches (to represent the pieces of fencing) as shown in the picture, to see how the farmer formed the six pens.

During one dark night someone stole one of the pieces of fencing. The farmer worked out that even with only twelve pieces of fencing he could still form six separate pens, each the same size.

Take one of your matches away and see if you can work out how the farmer solved the problem.

The answer is on page 126.

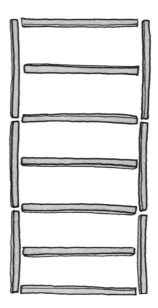

MATCH MENDING

YOU NEED:
- A handkerchief
- Two matches

Push a wooden matchstick into the hem of your handkerchief and you are ready to perform this baffling magic trick.

When the time comes to show the trick you take a match from its box and show it to your audience. Then you remove your handkerchief from your pocket and place the match into its centre.

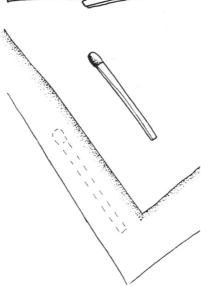

Fold the handkerchief around the match. There are, of course, two matches in the handkerchief now but the spectators are aware of only one. You must keep track of the hidden match.

Let someone feel the match (the secret one) through the folded material, then ask them to break the match in two. Everyone must be absolutely certain that the match has been broken.

Now shake out the handkerchief and the other match will fall out as if it has been completely restored! The broken match remains hidden in the hem.

YOU NEED:
- A coin
- A long length of cotton thread
- Sticky tape

Use a small piece of sticky tape to attach the cotton to the coin. Place the coin on the ground and then unravel the

Runaway Coin

cotton to a hiding place nearby.

You now have to lie in wait until someone spots the coin and tries to pick it up. As their fingers are just about to touch the coin you pull the thread – the coin runs away from the person, much to their surprise and your amusement.

THE ELECTRIC COIN

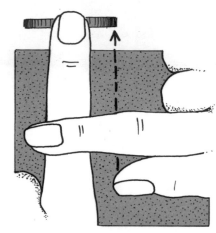

YOU NEED:
● A coin

Hold the coin on its edge on a table-top by pressing on it with your left first finger.

You now rub your finger with the first finger of the right hand. As you do this you tell everyone that you are trying to generate an electric current through your fingers.

Suddenly move your right forefinger along the full length of your left finger and off the end of the nail. This causes the coin to spin rapidly on the table.

What your friends do not see is the fact that your right thumb tip actually causes the coin to spin. As your right finger passes the coin, the tip of the right thumb hits the edge of the coin. It is trickery, not electricity, that makes the coin spin.

MAKING MONEY

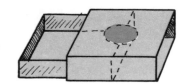

YOU NEED:
● An empty matchbox
● A coin

Before showing the trick to anyone, secretly hide the coin between the top of the matchbox drawer and the cover of the box. The dotted lines in the picture show the position of the hidden coin.

Keep the box open and say to your friends, "This is how a magician makes money."

Borrow a coin from someone and place it in the box. Close the box and the secret coin will drop into the drawer to join the borrowed coin.

Wave your hands over the box and then open it. Everyone will be amazed to see that the single coin has multiplied into two!

MAKING MORE MONEY

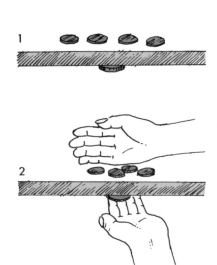

YOU NEED:
● Five coins
● Soap

This is another way to show how a magician can make money.

You place four coins in a row along the edge of a table. Then you show that your hands are empty before scooping the coins off the table. When you show the coins again there are now five!

Unbeknown to the people watching, the fifth coin is secretly added to the others as you scoop them off the table. The extra coin is concealed under the table-top. A small pellet of wet soap holds the coin in place (1).

As you scoop the coins off the table, the fingers of the hand waiting to receive the coins slip beneath the table-top and take the extra coin as well (2).

Like all magic, you should practise this trick in private until you can do it smoothly.

72

VANISHING COIN

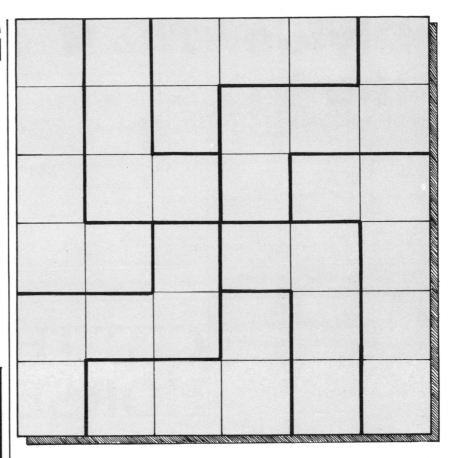

SQUARE THE SHAPE

YOU NEED:
- A handkerchief or cloth napkin
- A coin

You show a coin on your outstretched palm and then cover it with a handkerchief. You then allow several people to feel under the handkerchief to make sure the coin is still there. Suddenly, you whisk the handkerchief away and the coin has vanished!

This trick will gain you the reputation of being able to perform difficult sleight of hand. But all you need is a friend to be your secret assistant.

Your friend is the last person to feel beneath the handkerchief. He pretends to feel the coin but he actually takes it away. All you now have to do is act like a real magician and impress your audience with your skill.

YOU NEED:
- A sheet of thin card
- A pen or pencil
- Scissors

On a sheet of thin card, draw a block of thirty-six squares as shown in the picture.

Draw in the darker lines, as shown, and then cut along them. You will now have eight shapes, which you hand to someone with the request that the pieces are to be arranged in the shape of a square.

This one is guaranteed to have your friends scratching their heads for quite a time!

Divide the L

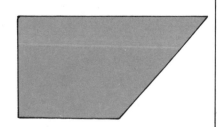

YOU NEED:
- Paper and a pencil

Copy this L shape on to a piece of paper and then see if you can divide it into four smaller L shapes, all the same size as each other.

The answer is on page 126.

TWELVE TRIANGLES

YOU NEED:
- Paper and a pencil

Copy this shape on to a piece of paper. Can you now divide it into twelve triangles all the same size?

The answer is on page 127.

THE 'H' PUZZLE

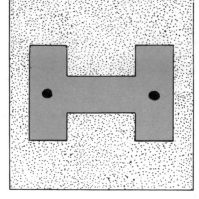

YOU NEED:
- Paper and a pencil

Copy this letter H on to a piece of paper. Can you now divide it into four pieces, each the same shape and size? The dividing lines should touch one or both of the two dots.

The answer is on page 126.

CUT THE HORSESHOE

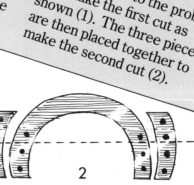

YOU NEED:
- Paper and a pencil
- Scissors

Draw the horseshoe below on a sheet of paper and then cut it out. Now hand it to a friend and tell her that the 14 dots represent nails.

The problem is to cut the horseshoe into seven pieces, in such a way that each piece contains two nails. There is just one stipulation – she is only allowed to make two straight cuts.

It is a good idea to have several horseshoes cut out ready, for it is quite likely that your friend will cut up quite a few before giving up.

The answer to the problem is to make the first cut as shown (1). The three pieces are then placed together to make the second cut (2).

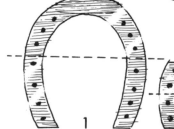

1   2

74

YOU NEED:

- An envelope
- A sheet of card
- A pen or pencil
- Scissors

One of the most famous magical tricks ever done is sawing a lady in half without causing her any harm. Here is a way that you can perform a version of this trick and convince your friends that you are a great magician.

Take a long envelope, seal it, and cut a small piece from each end so that you have a paper tube. On the back of the envelope make two cuts, as shown (1), through the back of the envelope only.

Now draw 'the lady' on a sheet of card and cut it out. If you cannot draw, you could cut a full-length picture from a magazine and stick that on the card instead.

Show the lady to your audience and slide it into the magic cabinet (the envelope). In doing this you must make sure that it comes out at the first cut and re-enters the envelope through the second cut. Be careful that your spectators never see a rear view of the envelope or they will know how the trick is done.

Take a pair of scissors and, inserting one point between the lady and the envelope, as shown in the picture (2), cut the envelope in half.

Your audience believe that you must have cut the lady in two as well. But when you remove the envelope the lady is still in one piece! It must be magic.

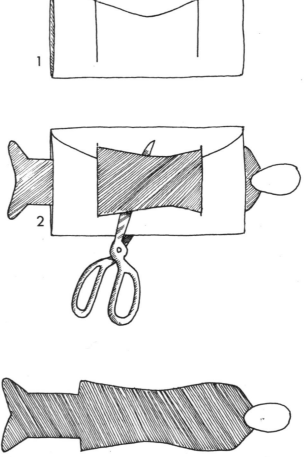

AN AMAZING MEMORY

YOU NEED:
- A pack of playing cards

Hand someone a pack of cards and ask him or her to shuffle them well. When the cards are given back to you, tell everyone you have an amazing memory and that you are going to try and remember the order of the cards.

Spread the cards before your eyes as if you are memorizing the order. In fact the only card you have to remember is the card at the bottom of the pack.

Now gather the cards together and hold them behind your back as you tell your audience you have memorized every card. While the cards are behind your back, secretly lift off about one third of the cards, turn them over and place them back on the pack.

Now bring the cards forward in your right hand, with the bottom card facing the audience (this is the card you remembered earlier). Call out the name of this card. At the same time take note of the card that is facing you (because you turned some cards over, part of the pack is facing one way and the rest is facing the other way).

Take the cards behind your back and remove the bottom card (the one you have just named) and throw it on the table.

Turn the whole pack over and bring it forward once again. The card you saw a few seconds ago is now facing the audience. Name this card and look at the one facing you.

Once again, take the cards behind your back, remove the named card and throw it on the table, turn the whole pack over and bring your hand to the front again.

Again you know the identity of the card the audience can see, which you name, and the card facing you will be the next one in the sequence.

Keep going like this until you find a back of a card facing you. All the rest of the cards are facing the same way so you must stop at this point. But, by this time, you will have named enough cards to convince the audience that you really did memorize the whole pack.

With practice you will be able to do this whole sequence of actions so fast that you can almost name the 'memorized' cards faster than the audience can see them!

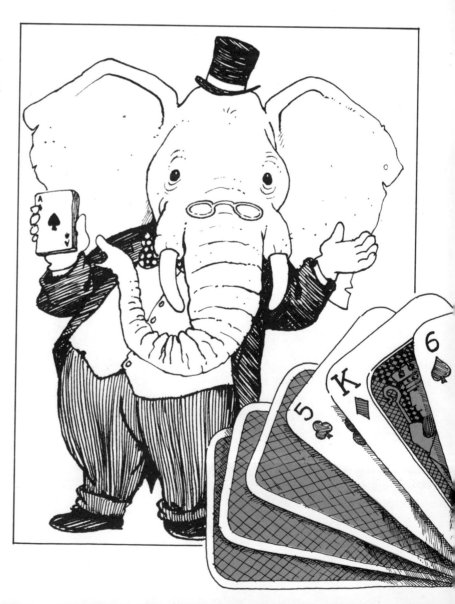

COUNTING THE CARDS

YOU NEED:
- A pack of playing cards

This is a good card trick to baffle your friends – but you will need to do a little advance preparation before you can show it.

Arrange 13 playing cards in the following order: Five, Nine, Ten, King, Jack, Two, Four, Six, Queen, Ace, Seven, Eight, Three. It doesn't matter which suits they are.

Place these 13 cards back on the top of the pack so that the Five is now the top card. Put the pack back in its case.

When the right time comes to perform the trick, remove the cards from the case and count 13 cards from the top of the pack on to the table. This actually reverses the order of the cards so the top card of the pile on the table is the Three.

Pick up the 13 cards and count "A, C, E," placing one card to the bottom of the pile as you call out each letter. Drop the next card face up on the table – it will be the Ace.

Now count out "T, W, O," again moving a card to the bottom of the pile as each letter is called. The next card is placed face up on the table – it is the Two.

Then count out "T, H, R, E, E," and the next card will be the Three.

Continue in this way until all the cards you have counted are lying face up on the table.

LIFT THAT LEG

Stand with the whole of your right side pressing against a wall. It is important that your right heel, leg, side, arm, shoulder and head are all touching the wall.

Now try to lift your left leg out and upwards without moving any part of your body away from the wall. Not easy, is it!

MULTIPLYING LEGS

1 × 4 = 7

"How can you leave the room with two legs and come back with six?" That is the question you ask a friend.

It is a problem that may puzzle your friend, but all he has to do is go out of the room, pick up the family dog or cat and then walk back in again.

If the cat is out or the dog is too heavy then a chair will do just as well. Whatever your friend chooses, he has gone out of the room with two legs and come back with six.

If your friend is unable to come up with the solution to this problem you will have to show off your superiority by doing it yourself.

NOSE MEASUREMENT

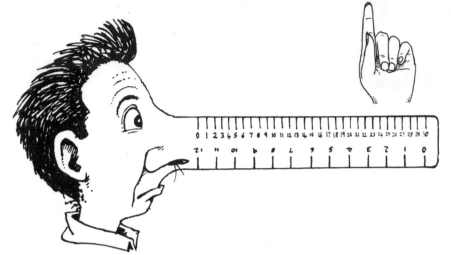

It has been said that the length of the first two joints of a person's forefinger is exactly the same as the length of his or her nose.

If you tell people this they are liable to scoff but you can prove that it is true. Get your friends to hold out a forefinger and then place their thumb on the second joint as shown. If they place the finger on their nose with the thumb tip touching the end of the nose they will find that the statement is true.

Hand Calendar

If you ever have trouble remembering the number of days in each month you could try this method.

Close both your hands into fists and hold them with the backs of the hands towards you. Now look at the picture and you will see how the knuckles and the spaces between them can be used to represent the twelve months of the year.

Each of the months indicated by the knuckles have 31 days in them. The months indicated by the spaces have 30 days. There is just one exception to this rule and that is February, which has 28 days (29 in a leap year).

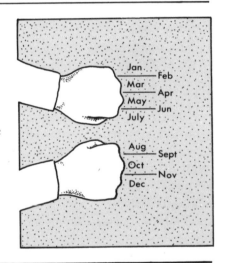

FINGER LICKIN' GOOD

YOU NEED:
- A bread stick

Imagine the surprise of your friends when, after saying you are a little bit hungry, you pull off one of your fingers and eat it all up!

Break off a piece of bread stick the same length as one of your fingers. Hold it by squeezing it between your second and third fingers.

When the time is right to perform the stunt you hold up your hand (not for too long or your friends will spot that you have too many fingers), break off what appears to be the middle finger and then eat it!

PUZZLING PARASOL

YOU NEED:
- Paper and a pencil
- Scissors

Copy this parasol shape (1) on to the paper and cut it out.

Can you now cut the parasol with just two straight cuts, in such a way that the pieces can be arranged to form the shape of a rectangle, as shown (2)?

The answer is on page 126.

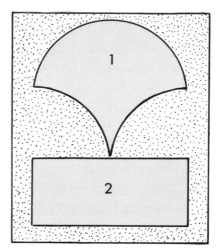

YOU NEED:
- Paper and pencil
- Scissors

Copy this letter N on a piece of paper and then cut it out.

Can you now make one cut in such a way that the two pieces can be arranged to form the letter M?

The answer is on page 127.

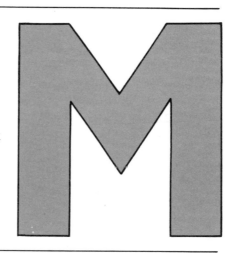

Paper Weights

OU NEED:
- Two pieces of paper
- A pen or pencil

Write the word 'light' on one piece of paper and the word 'heavy' on the other piece. Tell everyone that you will drop both pieces of paper at exactly the same time, but

HEAVY

that the 'light' one will reach the floor last because the other one is 'heavy'.

They will not believe you. What you have said is, however, absolutely true – the 'heavy' paper does fall to the floor faster than the 'light' paper – because you screw the 'heavy' paper into a ball before you drop it!

79

TRICKY RECTANGLE

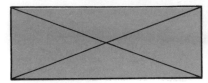

YOU NEED:
● Paper and a pencil

Draw this rectangle with its two diagonals on a sheet of paper. Now challenge someone to draw exactly the same diagram – but without lifting the pen or pencil from the paper and without going over any line twice.

Your friend is bound to give up eventually because it is actually impossible! It is very likely that your friend will actually turn the challenge back on you. In fact, you can do it – even though it is impossible – by means of a neat little trick.

Take the paper and fold the bottom edge up (A). Now draw the first of the short sides of the rectangle (line 1), starting at the top and moving the pencil towards yourself. Continue the line over the folded part of the paper, as shown. With the pencil still on the folded part of the paper draw line 2 across to the other short side, then upwards to draw the line marked 3.

Unfold the paper without lifting your pencil. You can now easily finish the drawing by following the arrows (4, 5, 6 and 7) in the sequence shown in the picture (B).

YOU NEED:
● Paper and pencil

"Can you draw a circle, complete with a dot in its centre, without lifting your pen or pencil from the paper?" That is the impossible challenge you put to your friends and it is very unlikely that they will be able to work out how to do it.

You, of course, can do it. This is how. Take a piece of paper and fold the top right corner inwards. Draw a dot on the main part of the paper at the place where the corner of the paper touches. Then run your pencil from the dot on to the folded portion of the paper, to what will be the edge of the circle.

CENTRE POINT

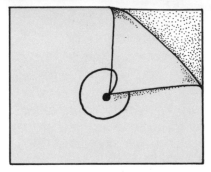

Continue drawing the circle and fold the corner back to complete it. You have now drawn a circle with a dot on its centre and your pencil never left the paper.

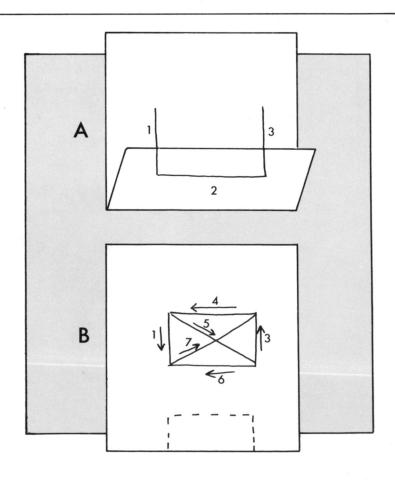

THE BOUNCING HANDKERCHIEF

YOU NEED:
- A small rubber ball
- An elastic band
- A handkerchief

Place the rubber ball on your handkerchief. Now put the elastic band around the ball and the material so that the ball is trapped in a little pocket hidden in the centre of the handkerchief.

While you are talking to someone take your handkerchief from your pocket and pretend to wipe your nose. Then throw the handkerchief to the ground. It will, of course, bounce back up into the air where you catch it. Place it back in your pocket as if bouncing handkerchiefs were the most ordinary thing in the world.

That should raise a few eyebrows and who knows, you could start a fashion!

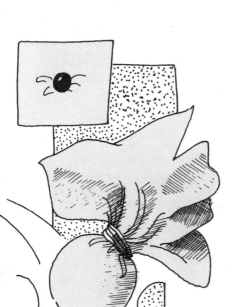

HOW TO MAKE METAL FLOAT

YOU NEED:
- A glass of water
- Tissue paper
- A sewing needle

Everyone knows that if you put a piece of metal into water it will sink. But you are such a clever person that you can make metal float.

This is how you do it. Place the needle on the paper and then gently put the paper on to the surface of the water. When the paper is saturated with water it will sink – leaving the needle floating on the surface.

You will find this trick is more successful if you rub the needle between the palms of your hands first. It picks up grease from your skin and this helps it to float. But be careful that you do not stick the needle into yourself when you [do t]his.

THE MAGNETIC BALL

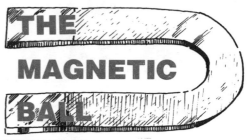

YOU NEED:
- A ping-pong ball
- Cotton
- Sticky tape

Show your friends a ping-pong ball to which is attached a length of cotton or thin string. The easiest way to attach the cotton to the ball is to use a piece of sticky tape.

Tell everyone that the ball is magnetic – but it is not attracted to metal like an ordinary magnet. This magnetic ball is attracted to water!

It sounds absolutely amazing and it is very likely that your friends will not believe you – until you show that it is true!

Allow the ball to hang against a stream of water flowing from a tap. The ball will cling to the water as if it is magnetized. Maybe you were telling the truth after all!

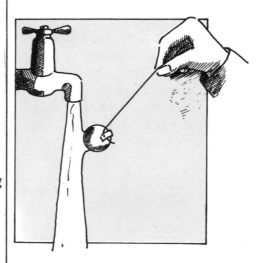

DISAPPEARING RIBBON

YOU NEED:
● A ping-pong ball
● A ribbon

You show everyone a piece of coloured ribbon and then push it into your closed fist. When you open your hand the ribbon has transformed itself into a ping-pong ball!

All you need for this neat little trick, apart from the ribbon and the ball, is a knife to cut a hole in the ball. Be very careful that you do not cut a hole in yourself!

Hide the ball in one hand as you show the ribbon in your other hand. Push the ribbon into your closed fist and into the ball. Make a magic pass over it with your hand and the ribbon appears to have changed into the ball!

Make sure that you keep the hole in the ball well hidden from your audience.

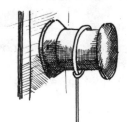

YOU NEED:
● A cup
● A piece of string
● Scissors

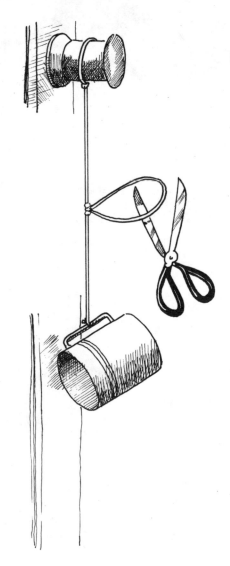

Tie the cup to a door handle with the piece of string. The string should be about 75 cm long.

Now challenge someone to cut the string at the centre in such a way that the cup will not crash to the floor. They are not allowed to touch either the string or the cup after the cut has been made.

When your friend gives up you show how it is done. All you have to do is to knot the centre part of the string into a loop, making sure that the knot is tight as you do so. Now all you have to do is cut the string at the centre of the loop – and the cup will stay hanging where it is.

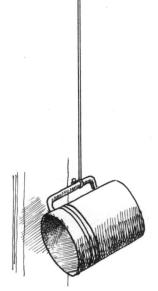

TOUCH THEM ALL

YOU NEED:
- Six drinking straws or pencils

Can you place six drinking straws on a table in such a way that each straw is touching *all* the other straws?

You can if you arrange them as shown in the drawing.

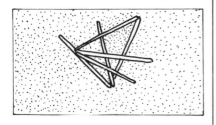

PORTRAIT PROBLEM

A girl and her father were in a room looking at the portrait of a man.

The girl said to her father, "That man's mother was my mother's mother-in-law."

What relation is the girl to the person in the portrait?

The answer is on page 125.

ANOTHER PORTRAIT PROBLEM

A lady was looking at a portrait of a man when she said, "I do not have any brothers or sisters, but that man's mother was my mother's child."

What relation is the lady to the man in the picture?

The answer is on page 125.

WHAT DAY IS IT?

When the day after tomorrow is yesterday, today will be as far after Sunday as today was before Sunday when the day before yesterday was tomorrow.

What day is it today?

The answer is on page 127.

COIN DROP

YOU NEED:
- A coin
- A piece of paper

Show your friends the coin and a small piece of paper roughly the same size as the coin.

Now say, "If I were to drop this coin and this paper at exactly the same time from the same height, which one would hit the ground first?"

Naturally everyone will say that the coin will land first, because the paper will simply float gently to the ground. You can now prove your friends wrong, for when you drop the coin and the paper the paper lands first!

How do you do it? That's simple, all you have to do is place the coin on top of the paper and then drop them together. They will fall together, but as the paper is underneath the coin it is bound to reach the ground first.

The Travelling Aces

You show an Ace of Spades and place it in a small box on the left of the table. An Ace of Hearts is placed in a box on the right.

You then make a magic sign and remove the Ace of Spades from the box on the right and the Ace of Hearts has now travelled across to the box on the left.

What you do not tell your audience is that the Ace of Spades has an Ace of Hearts from another pack glued to its back, and the Ace of Hearts has an Ace of Spades glued to its back. To make it appear that the Aces have changed places, all you have to do is secretly turn them over in the box before taking them out.

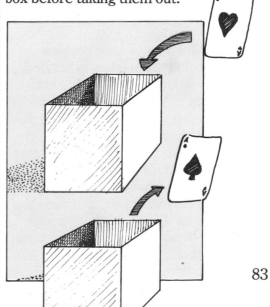

83

I'm Forever Blowing Bubbles

YOU NEED:
- Washing-up liquid
- Water
- Sugar

Fancy blowing some bubbles but you can't afford to buy some bubble solution? Then try this.

Pour some washing-up liquid into a cup.

Add an equal amount of water. Put in a spoonful of sugar and mix well.

You will find this makes a great solution for blowing bubbles.

YOU NEED:
- A paper clip or fuse wire

One way to form bubbles using the solution described on this page is to use a bubble ring. You can make one quite easily by bending a paper clip or some thick fuse wire into the shape of a circle.

Dip the ring into the solution until a film of the soapy water forms across the ring. Wave the ring through the air or blow on it gently and you have become a champion bubble blower!

FIND THE ACES

YOU NEED:
- A pack of playing cards
- A paper clip
- A safety pin

You hand someone a pack of cards and ask them to shuffle the cards. The pack is then handed back to you. You hold the cards behind your back and bring out the four Aces, one at a time.

To your audience this feat of magic is absolutely amazing, for the cards have been thoroughly shuffled and, with the cards behind your back, you could not see what you were doing.

What the audience do not know is that the Aces were never in the pack to start with! Before showing this trick you secretly remove the Aces. Place these four cards in a paper clip and then pin the paper clip inside the back of your jacket or jersey with a safety pin.

When the cards have been shuffled and you are holding the pack behind your back, you pull the four Aces from their secret hiding place and then bring them forward, one at a time.

THE VANISHING KEY

YOU NEED:
- A key
- A piece of elastic
- A safety pin

Tie the key to the piece of elastic (you will have to experiment to find the correct length). The other end of the elastic is tied to the safety pin.

Attach the pin to the inside of your jacket sleeve. Put the jacket on and pull the key down the sleeve to your hand.

You now hand the key to someone, but as that person goes to take it you let go of the key. The elastic then pulls the key right back up your sleeve, but to your friend it seems that the key has vanished by magic.

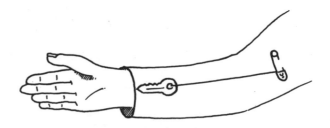

Off With His Shirt

This is a great stunt for a party. You ask for a boy to help you. You then unfasten the buttons of his shirt at the neck and the cuffs. Then you place your hand to the rear of your friend's neck, grasp the shirt collar and pull. Much to everyone's surprise you pull his shirt off completely!

The person you get to help in this trick has secretly put his shirt on in a special way before the start of the performance. The shirt is draped over his back as shown in the picture. Only his neck and his wrists are actually in the shirt, but when your friend puts his jacket on the shirt will look quite normal.

All you have to do is undo the buttons and pull. It looks absolutely amazing.

MUSCLES

YOU NEED:
- A glass of water

Tell your friends that you are the strongest person in the world. To prove your claim you hold a glass of water in your left hand and get a friend to hold your left forearm with both his hands.

You now say that no matter how strongly your friend holds your arm you will be able to lift the glass to your mouth and drink the water. As you are saying this try to lift your arm against your friend's strength.

Keep the struggle going for a little while (make sure you do not spill the water over the carpet) and everyone will think that your friend is winning.

Now take the glass with your *right* hand and lift it up to your mouth!

COUNTER MOVES

YOU NEED:
- Paper and a pencil
- Three silver coins
- Three copper coins

Copy this diagram on to a sheet of paper. Now place the three silver coins on the squares 2, 3 and 4 and the three copper coins on the squares 5, 6 and 7.

The problem is now to change the positions of the coins, so the silver coins are moved down to where the copper coins are and the copper coins are moved up to the positions originally occupied by the silver coins.

Here are the rules. The coins must be moved alternately – first a silver coin, then a copper coin, and so on. They can move in any direction – horizontally, vertically or diagonally – but only one square at a time and only to an unoccupied square.

See how many moves it takes you.

The answer is on page 127.

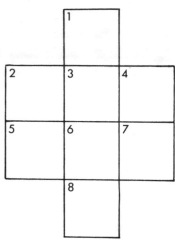

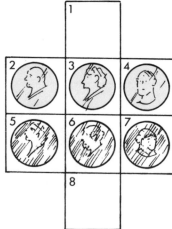

YOU NEED:
- Paper and pencil
- Two silver coins
- Two copper coins

ALL CHANGE

Draw this diagram on a piece of paper. Draw it as large as you can. Now place two copper coins on the numbers 3 and 8 and two silver coins on the numbers 5 and 10.

Your problem is now to get the coins to the opposite ends of the design so that the copper coins are on 5 and 10 and the silver coins end up on 3 and 8.

The rules for doing this are that the coins can be moved only in straight lines and are allowed to stop only on the circles. And at no time must there be a silver coin and a copper coin on a straight line with one another. There is no need to move the silver and copper coins alternately if you do not wish to do so.

So put your thinking cap on and off you go.

The answer is on page 127.

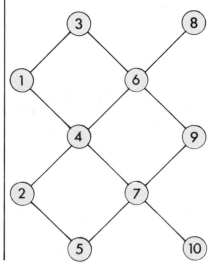

Nine Dots and Four Lines

YOU NEED:
- Paper and pencil

On a piece of paper draw nine dots in three rows each of three dots, as shown.

Can you now draw just four straight lines that will join up all the dots? In doing this you are not allowed to lift your pen or pencil from the paper, or to draw over any line twice.

The answer is on page 127.

YOU NEED:
- A set of dominoes

With only a set of dominoes you can appear to predict what is going to happen before it does.

The audience is given a set of dominoes and asked to arrange them on the table as if they were playing a normal game. When they have laid out all the dominoes they will look something like the set shown on this page.

Ask everyone to note the numbers at each end of the domino pattern (in the picture these are a four and a two). You now draw attention to a folded slip of paper that has been resting on the table right from the start. When the paper is opened it reveals a message you wrote earlier, 'The two end dominoes will be a four and a two' (or whatever the end numbers happen to be). As this is absolutely correct it seems that you must be able to predict the future.

How did you know what to write on the paper before the start of the trick? The secret is that when no one was looking you took one of the dominoes out of the set. The numbers on that domino are the numbers that will be at the ends of the row when all the other dominoes are laid out. So, if the domino you take has a three and a six on it, that is what you write on the paper. In our example the missing domino was a four and a two — and you can see how that worked out.

Domino Prediction

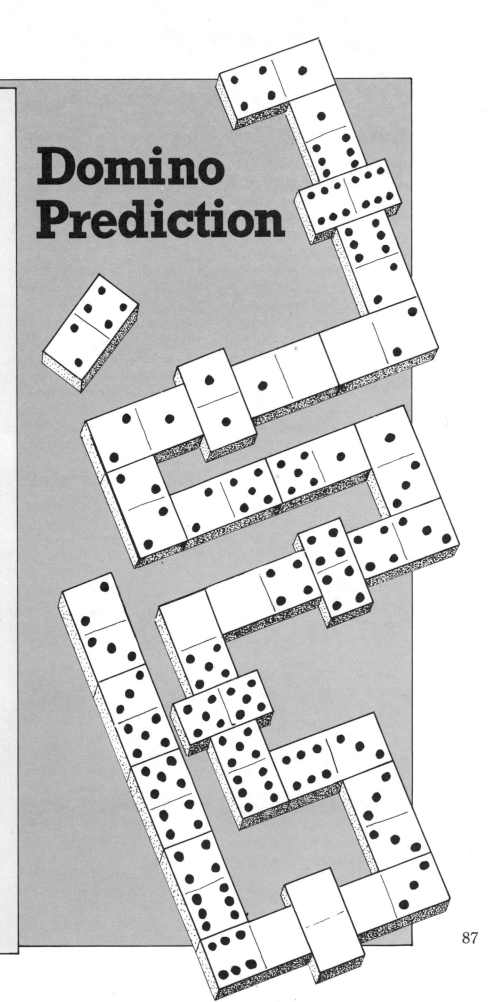

YOU NEED:
- A pack of cards
- An envelope
- A pen and paper

Before showing this trick, take a look at the ninth card down from the top of a pack of cards. Let us suppose that it is the Queen of Hearts.

On a piece of paper write 'You will choose the Queen of Hearts' (or whatever the ninth card was). Seal this piece of paper in an envelope and you are ready to perform the trick.

Place the sealed envelope on the table and then show the pack of cards. Ask someone to say any number between ten and twenty. You then count that number of cards, one at a time, from the top of the pack and place them on the table face down.

You then point out that the chosen number consists of two digits. Add these two digits together (if, for example, the chosen number was 17 you would add one and seven to get eight) and deal this number of cards, one at a time, from the pile you have just dealt and place them back on the pack.

Take the next card from the pile and place it face down on the table. Ask someone to open the sealed envelope and read your message. The card on the table is the very card that you said would be chosen!

This trick works because when the digits of any number between ten and twenty are added together and then taken away from the chosen number the answer will always be nine.

YOU NEED:
- A pack of cards

Have someone shuffle a pack of cards until they are certain that they are well mixed up. Get another person to take out a few cards (face down) from the pack.

You now hold these cards in front of a third person with the request that she thinks of just

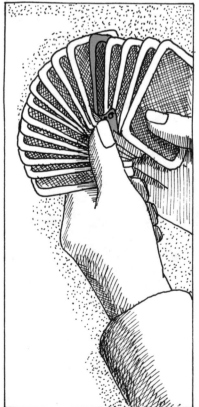

one of the cards. The cards have their backs towards you so you cannot see which is which. When the person has chosen a card ask her to point to it so everyone else can see which card she has in mind.

Even though you have not seen any of the cards you can now read her mind and tell her the card she is thinking of.

If you look at the picture you will see how you know the identity of the chosen card. As soon as your friend points to it you secretly bend up the corner of the card. No one will see you do this as the cards hide this crafty action.

As you now know which card has been chosen, you can pretend to read your friend's mind.

QUICK CHANGE CARD

YOU NEED:
- Three playing cards
- Glue

You show your friends a playing card – it is the Ace of Spades. You then brush your hand over the face of the card and it changes to the King of Hearts?

For this trick you will need to make a special card. Take three old playing cards and fold two of them in half. In the picture these are shown as the Ace of Spades and the King of Hearts, but any two cards will do just as well.

Now glue the two folded cards together and to the face of the third card, as shown. You now have a card with a moveable flap. If the flap is up the card is the Ace of Spades and if it is down the card showing is the King of Hearts.

To perform the trick, you show the card with the flap up. Then bring your hand down across the face of the card and move the flap down. Your hand hides the movement of the flap and the card seems to change like magic.

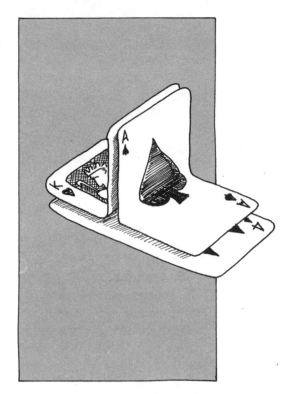

WHICH HAND?

YOU NEED:
- A coin

One of your friends is asked to hide a coin, or other small object, in one of his hands while your back is turned.

You then ask him to hold the hand containing the coin against his forehead and to think hard as to whether it is his left hand or his right hand.

The object of this is to transmit his brain waves to you so that you can read his mind. After a few minutes you say that you have received the message and that you now know which hand holds the coin. Ask him to lower his hand, and hold both hands out with the coin still concealed.

You then turn around and tell everyone which hand is holding the coin.

You do this, not by mind-reading but by simply taking a quick look at your helper's hands. The one which holds the coin will be paler than the other because the blood will have run from it while it was held against his forehead.

THE MAGIC BANGLE

YOU NEED:
- A large sheet of coloured paper
- A plastic bangle
- A square of card
- Scissors and glue

Resting on your table is a large sheet of coloured paper. On the paper there is the bangle and the square of card.

You borrow a coin from someone and place it on the paper. Then you show the card, place it on top of the bangle, and lift the two together to place them over the coin. When the card is lifted the coin has vanished.

You then replace the card on top of the bangle. When you lift up the card and bangle together the coin has reappeared.

To do this trick you have to prepare the bangle in a special way. All you have to do is glue one side of it to a piece of paper that matches the sheet of paper you place on the table. The edges of the paper have to be carefully trimmed so that no pieces project beyond the bangle.

The square of card that you use should be just large enough to cover the whole of the bangle.

If you now do the trick exactly as described it will work automatically. The audience think they can see through the bangle to the paper, but the paper glued to the bangle actually covers the coin and hides it from view.

WHERE IS THE COIN?

YOU NEED:
- A coin
- Three identical beakers or cups
- A hair
- Sticky tape or soap

You place a coin on the table and ask someone to cover it with a beaker that is also on the table. There are two more identical beakers on the table and you ask that these are placed next to the one hiding the coin, so there is no way that you can tell which beaker hides the coin. You have turned your back while all this is going on, but when you turn back round you can say immediately which of the three beakers covers the coin.

This trick is accomplished by means of a long hair attached to the coin. You can stick the hair to the coin with sticky tape or a small piece of wet soap.

When you turn to look at the beakers you are really looking for the hair sticking out from one of them and that will tell you the position of the hidden coin.

The Mystic Nine

YOU NEED:
- Twelve coins

Arrange the coins on a table so they form the shape of a

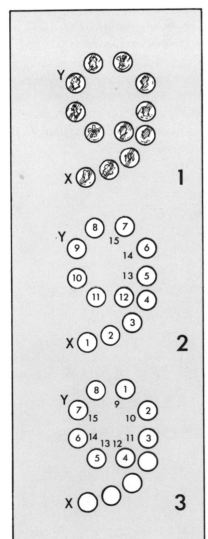

number nine as shown (1). Now ask someone to think of a number. This can be any number provided that it is greater than the number of the coins in the tail of the nine (over four).

While your back is turned your friend starts counting from the lowermost coin (marked X). The count goes around the body of the nine, in an anticlockwise direction, and continues around the circle only until the chosen number is reached.

Next, your friend is asked to count out his selected number again, starting from the last coin touched on the original count, but this time going around the circle (ignoring the tail) in a clockwise direction.

Although your back has been turned during all this counting you can tell everyone on which coin the last count finished. You can do this quite easily because it is the same coin every time!

With twelve coins arranged as shown here, in the first illustration, the count will always end on the coin marked Y. Here is an example. If the number chosen was 15 the first count will be as shown in diagram 2. Diagram 3 shows the second count (starting from the last coin of the first count) and it ends on coin Y. Try it with some other numbers and you will see that it works every time.

The trick will actually work with any number of coins but you will have to experiment to discover which is the finishing coin in each case.

ALPHABETIC CODE

Here is another code you can use for secret messages. First write out the alphabet and then put the same letters underneath – but in reverse order – like this:

A B C D E F G H I
Z Y X W V U T S R

J K L M N O P Q R
Q P O N M L K J I

S T U V W X Y Z
H G F E D C B A

You write your message using the substitute letters instead of the real letters. So, the word SECRET would become HVXIVG. Your friend would be able to understand the message by using the same type of table as you.

Here is a message using this code. Can you work out what it says?

SVIV RH Z NVHHZTV FHRMT GSRH XLWV. WL MLG OVG ZM VMVNB ZTVMG PMLD SLD GSV XLWV RH DLIPVW LFG.

Crossword Code

If you want to send secret messages to a friend without anyone else being able to crack the code then try the Crossword Code.

To use this code both you and your friend have to have a copy of an identical crossword grid. You can copy the one shown here, but it will be more secret if you make up your own.

When you want to write a secret message, you first write the letters in on the crossword, going across the rows. Then you copy out the message on to a sheet of paper, but taking the letters running downwards.

When your secret friend receives the message he reverses the process. He takes his crossword grid and copies the message on to it, working downwards. When the complete message is written on the grid he can read it quite easily by reading across the rows.

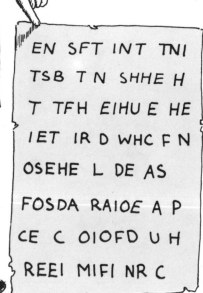

THROUGH THE HOLE

YOU NEED:
- Paper and a pen
- Scissors

This is a very good way to send secret messages for they are impossible to read without a special device.

This device simply consists of a sheet of paper or card with several oblong holes cut in it. You will need two of these, both exactly the same, one for you and one for the person who is going to receive the messages.

To write a secret message, you put the cut out card on a sheet of paper of the same size and write your letter in the holes. Now take the cut out card away and write lots of other words on the paper.

The letter now makes no sense whatsoever and no one but your friend, who has a cut out card the same as yours, will be able to read it.

To read the letter all your friend has to do is place her cut out card on the letter and read the words that show through the holes.

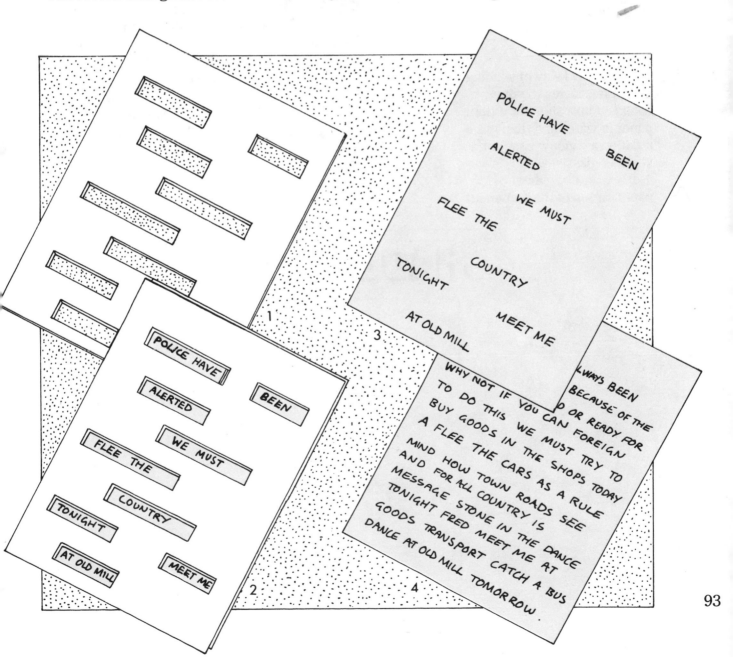

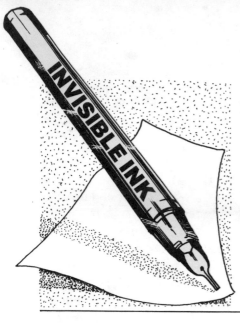

YOU NEED:
- Lemon juice
- A fine brush
- A sheet of paper

Every secret agent should know how to make invisible ink. There are in fact lots of ways to do this, but the simplest is to use ordinary lemon juice.

Squeeze some lemon juice into a bowl and use a fine brush or pointed stick to write your message. Allow the paper to dry and the writing will be completely invisible.

To make the writing appear place the paper on a hot radiator. As the heat from the radiator warms up the paper the writing will gradually appear until it can be read quite easily.

YOU NEED:
- Two sheets of writing paper
- A pencil

This is a good way of sending secret messages to your friends. Dip a sheet of writing paper in water and then place it flat on a window pane, or a sheet of glass.

Place another sheet of paper on top of the wet sheet

Water Writing

and write your message on the top sheet with a pencil. It is important that you press hard when doing the writing.

Throw the top sheet away. The writing will be visible on the wet sheet, but when it dries out the writing will not be seen.

To make the writing visible again all your secret agent friend has to do is to immerse it in water once again.

SHADOW STAR

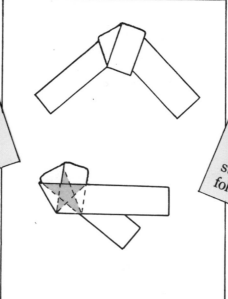

YOU NEED:
- Two long strips of paper

Hand someone one of the strips of paper and challenge him to fold the paper in such a way that a star is formed.

Even if your friend makes a star shape it will

not be very good – and he will find it difficult to do.

But you can do it quite easily. Take another strip of paper and simply tie a knot in it. Press the knot flat and then hold the paper up to the light. The shadow of a five-pointed star will be visible through the folds of the paper.

STAR TRICK

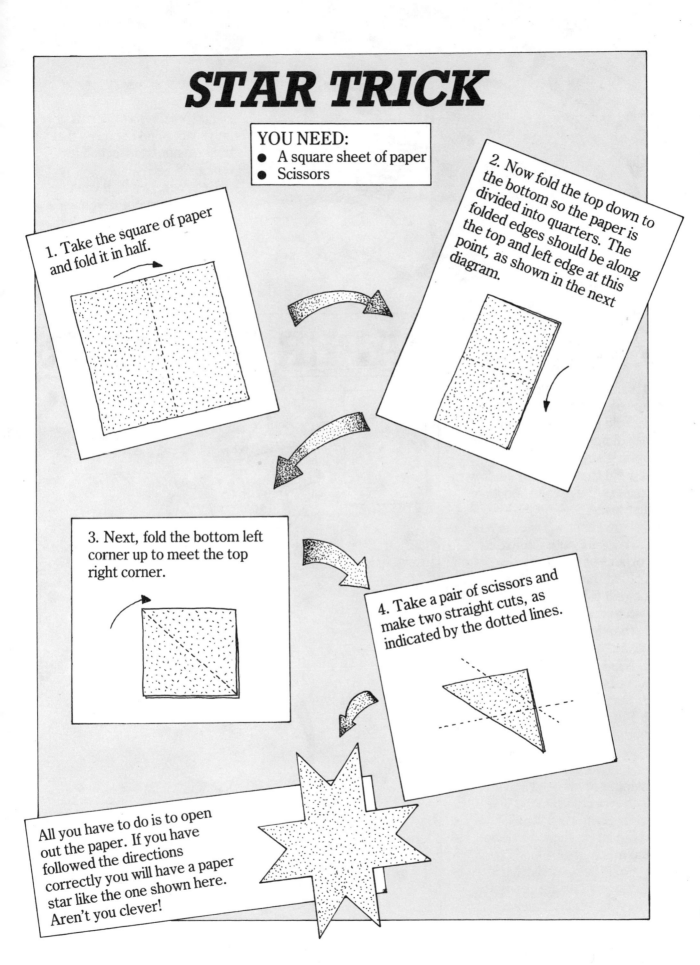

YOU NEED:
- A square sheet of paper
- Scissors

1. Take the square of paper and fold it in half.

2. Now fold the top down to the bottom so the paper is divided into quarters. The folded edges should be along the top and left edge at this point, as shown in the next diagram.

3. Next, fold the bottom left corner up to meet the top right corner.

4. Take a pair of scissors and make two straight cuts, as indicated by the dotted lines.

All you have to do is to open out the paper. If you have followed the directions correctly you will have a paper star like the one shown here. Aren't you clever!

FOLD IT

Hand someone a sheet of newspaper and bet them that they cannot fold it in half ten times.

Believe it or not, it can't be done. Up to about seven folds is fairly easy, but after that it becomes more difficult and by about the ninth or tenth fold it just cannot be done. Try it out yourself and see.

PAPER SNAPPER

YOU NEED:
● An oblong piece of paper

This neat device can make quite a loud noise.

1. Fold the sheet of paper in half along its length and then open it out again.
2. Fold the four corners down to meet the crease you have just made.
3. Now fold the paper in half once again, with the folded corners on the inside.
4. Find the centre of the longest side by folding it in two to make a crease. Unfold it, then fold the bottom corner up, as shown.
5. Next, you fold the top corner down.
6. Turn the whole thing over.
7. Fold the bottom point up to meet the top point.

With the longest side uppermost, take hold of your snapper at one end and swing it downwards rapidly. The force of the air will make part of the inner section fold out and make quite a loud crack.

Fold the open flap back inside and you are ready to use your snapper again.

96

PAPER SCREECHER

YOU NEED:
- A long, narrow strip of paper

Take the strip of paper and hold it taut between your thumbs, as shown in the picture.

Place your mouth against the slight opening between your thumbs and blow. With practice you will be able to produce a high-pitched screeching noise.

This also works using a blade of grass or a narrow leaf instead of the paper.

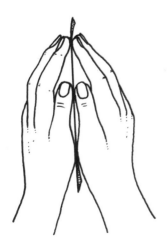

YOU NEED:
- A full, unopened bottle of lemonade

Challenge someone to take a drink from the bottle without opening it. Like many other things in this book, this sounds absolutely impossible. It should not be long before your friend says that it cannot be done.

You now show how clever you are by actually doing it! All you have to do is turn the bottle upside down, pour some liquid into the bowl-shaped base and then drink from that. You have taken a drink from the bottle without opening it.

Not all bottles have a hollow in the base so make sure you check your bottle before issuing your challenge.

DRINK IT UP

YOU NEED
- Paper
- A large bowl of water
- Cooking oil

Draw this fish shape on to a piece of paper and then cut it out. Cut a small hole in the middle of the body and then a thin slit running from the hole to the tail.

Carefully lay your fish on the surface of some water in a bath or a large bowl. It is important to remember that you should not let the top surface of the fish get wet when you do this.

Now pour a few drops of cooking oil in the central hole. Your fish should then move forward through the water, as if propelled by magic.

MAKE A MAGIC FISH

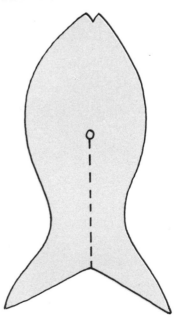

Cotton Caper

YOU NEED:
- A reel of cotton
- A needle

Get a reel of cotton that is of a different colour to the jacket you are wearing. Place the cotton reel in an inside pocket and then use a needle to push the end of the thread through your jacket.

Leave just a short piece of the thread showing on your jacket and sooner or later some kind person will try to pick it off for you.

As soon as they do so you walk away quickly – leaving your poor, unsuspecting friend holding a piece of cotton that is rapidly getting longer and longer!

JELLY EGG

YOU NEED:

- An egg
- Jelly mixture
- Paper and glue

For this amusing joke you will need some jelly mixture and a blown egg. If you do not know how to blow an egg take a look at page 59.

Make up the jelly mixture according to the instructions on the packet. When the mixture has cooled down (but before it has set) pour it into one of the holes in the egg (having sealed up the other hole first with a small piece of paper or sticky tape).

Getting the jelly mixture into the egg can prove a bit of a problem. Possibly the easiest way is to fold a piece of paper into a tight funnel through which you pour the mixture. This can be a bit mucky so make sure you do it over a plate or a bowl.

When the egg is full seal up the top hole. Now leave it until the jelly sets.

Having made the egg, what do you do with it? Well, there are quite a few things you can do. Here are a few ideas – but perhaps you can think up some of your own as well.

Put the jelly egg in the

fridge along with all the other eggs and wait for someone to try to use it. Or you could put the egg in your lunch box. Your friends will have quite a surprise when you peel what appears to be an ordinary boiled egg – and it turns out to be made of jelly.

Put one in someone else's lunch box and wait for their reaction when they peel it.

Ask your lunch guests if they would like some jelly after their meal and then serve them with jelly eggs. They will think you have gone crazy – until you tell them to peel their eggs.

YOU NEED

- Four matches
- A small coin, or button

Place the four matches on the table to form the shape of a glass. Into the glass put the coin, or button, as shown in the picture (1).

Now challenge a friend to get the coin out of the glass without touching the coin. To do this he is allowed to move two matches only and the glass shape must remain intact.

It is quite a problem and one that can keep people puzzling for hours. But before you challenge anyone to try it you had better know the answer yourself.

The diagrams opposite show you which two matches

OUT OF THE GLASS

to move and where to place them. After they have been moved the glass shape is still there (although it is now upside down) and the coin is outside the glass.

Simple when you know how, isn't it!

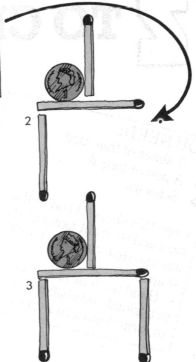

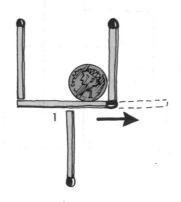

EVER CHANGING CARD

YOU NEED:
- A sheet of card
- A pen or pencil

You show a large playing card – the Ace of Diamonds. On the other side is the Four of Diamonds. When you turn it back to show the first side again it has become the Three of Diamonds. Turn it over again and it is the Six of Diamonds!

To do this trick you need a special card. It is easily made from a sheet of card and the pictures show everything you need to know – on side A there are two diamonds and on side B there are five diamonds as you can see.

The card appears to change because you can change the appearance of each side according to how you hold the card.

Hold side A with your hand covering the lower diamond and the card will look like an Ace. Turn the card over and place your hand over the middle diamond on the right so the card looks like a Four.

Turn the card over again, but this time your hand covers the blank space at the bottom, and the card looks like a Three. Turn the card over, with your hand covering the blank space, and it will look like a Six.

You should practise turning the card over and changing your hand positions until you can do it smoothly and without having to think.

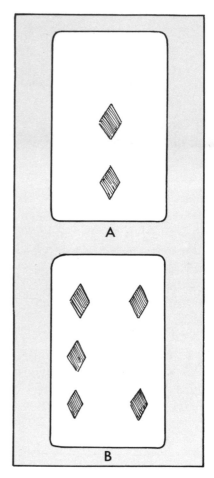

Z TO CROSS

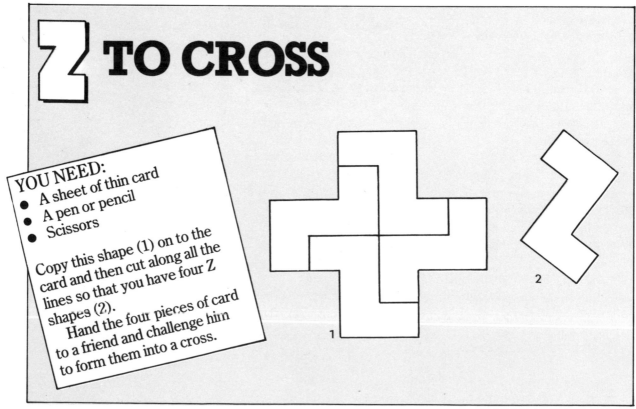

YOU NEED:
- A sheet of thin card
- A pen or pencil
- Scissors

Copy this shape (1) on to the card and then cut along all the lines so that you have four Z shapes (2).

Hand the four pieces of card to a friend and challenge him to form them into a cross.

CROSSED ARMS KNOT

YOU NEED:
- A piece of rope or string

Everyone knows that it is impossible to hold a piece of rope with one end in each hand and then to tie a knot in the rope without letting go of the ends.

It is just as well that no one told you it was impossible, because you can do it! This is how.

Lay the rope on a table. Now fold your arms. Keep your arms folded as you pick up one end of the rope in one hand and the other end of the rope in the other hand.

Keep tight hold of the rope and unfold your arms. There should now be a knot in the centre of the rope!

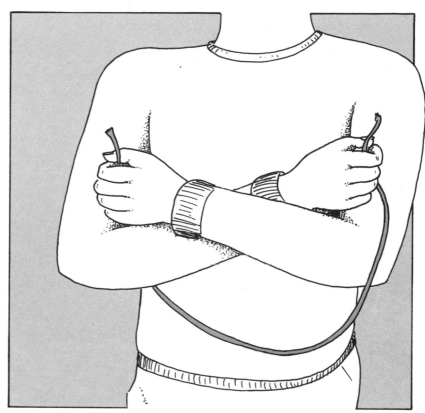

THE BROKEN NOSE

Place both of your hands over your nose as shown and grasp your nose between the finger and thumb of the uppermost hand. You now twist your nose from side to side. Each twist produces a loud crack from your nose.

It looks and sounds very effective and some of your friends will find your performance quite frightening. There is no need to let them know that the 'cracks' are produced by the lower hand hitting the thumbnail against your teeth!

CROSSED ARMS KNOT

Pocket Full of Lemonade

YOU NEED:
- A plastic bag
- Sticky tape

Next time you go into a café with your friends, or a restaurant with your family, take a strong plastic bag in your coat pocket.

Some time during your visit order a glass of lemonade (or whatever you like to drink).

When it is served, casually pour it into your pocket (and into the secret bag) as you say, "I'll save it for later." That should get you some strange looks!

Make sure you tape the bag into position before you try this or you will get even stranger looks as the lemonade seeps from your pocket and on to the floor!

THE KNOTTED HANDKERCHIEF

YOU NEED:
- A handkerchief

You give your handkerchief a shake and a knot appears in it. You can tell your friends that the knot was formed by magic, but in fact it was in the handkerchief all the time.

Before doing the trick you secretly tie a knot in one corner of your handkerchief.

Hold the handkerchief in one hand with the knot hidden

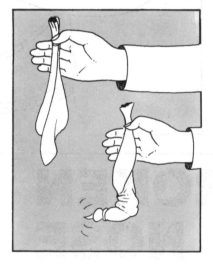

in that hand. Keep the knotted corner hidden as you bring the bottom (opposite) corner up to your hand. Now hold the handkerchief by both corners for a moment and then give it a shake. As you do this you release the knotted end of the material.

All you have really done is to change which end you are holding – but to everyone watching the knot seems to come from nowhere.

LINO CUT

The picture shows a piece of linoleum. How would you cut it so that it would fit a square room? Without, of course, spoiling the pattern.

The answer to this problem is really quite simple. Just cut the lino as shown. The two pieces will fit together to form a square and the pattern has not been affected.

102

DANCING HANKY

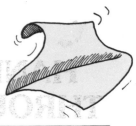

YOU NEED:
● A large handkerchief

Have you ever seen a handkerchief dance? No? Well you can if you follow these instructions.

Take the handkerchief and tie a knot in the middle of one side (1). Now take hold of the corners of the edge opposite the knot and twirl the handkerchief over and over (2). The more twists you can get into the handkerchief at this point the better (3).

Pass the end in the left hand to the right hand. Take hold of the end of the knot in the left hand. The knot represents the dancer's head and the two twisted sections being held by the right hand are the dancer's legs (4).

To make the dancer dance let go of one of the legs and pull on the other. The released leg will give a high kick and will spin round in a pirouette (5).

Now change your hold so that the other leg is released and the dancer will perform for you again!

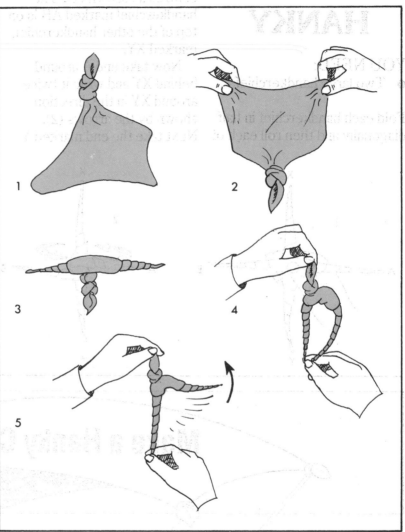

GLASS ON A CARD

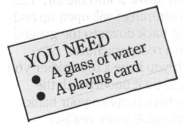

YOU NEED
● A glass of water
● A playing card

This is a good way of showing off your balancing skills. You take an ordinary playing card and then balance a glass tumbler on one edge of the card.

What your audience do not see is the fact that your forefinger is extended behind the card so that the glass is supported by the card and your finger.

You will find this easier to do if you bend the card just a little, first.

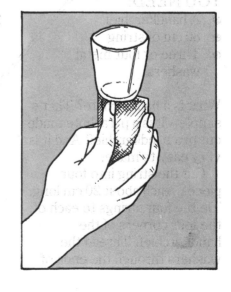

HANKY THROUGH HANKY

YOU NEED:
- Two large handkerchiefs

Fold each handkerchief in half diagonally and then roll each of them into a long, thin 'rope'.

Hold the two handkerchiefs in a cross formation at their centres as shown (1). The handkerchief marked AB is on top of the other handkerchief, marked XY.

Now take end A around behind XY and wrap it twice around XY in the direction shown by the arrows (2). Next take the end marked Y under AB and wrap it twice around AB as shown (3).

Bring your left hand underneath the handkerchiefs and take hold of the ends XY. The right hand takes hold of the ends AB from above.

Say a magic word and pull your hands apart. The handkerchiefs will melt through one another. It must be magic!

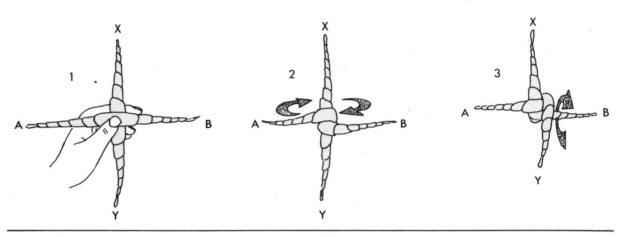

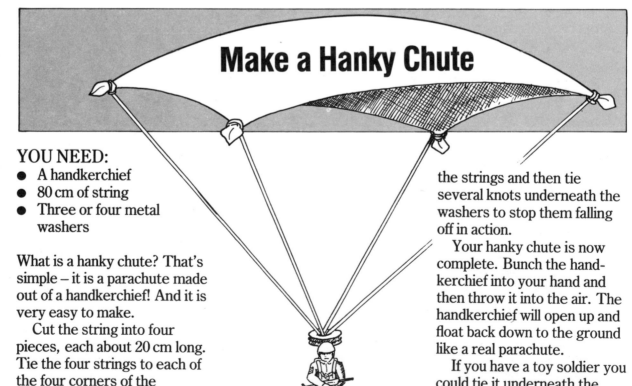

Make a Hanky Chute

YOU NEED:
- A handkerchief
- 80 cm of string
- Three or four metal washers

What is a hanky chute? That's simple – it is a parachute made out of a handkerchief! And it is very easy to make.

Cut the string into four pieces, each about 20 cm long. Tie the four strings to each of the four corners of the handkerchief. Thread the washers through the ends of the strings and then tie several knots underneath the washers to stop them falling off in action.

Your hanky chute is now complete. Bunch the handkerchief into your hand and then throw it into the air. The handkerchief will open up and float back down to the ground like a real parachute.

If you have a toy soldier you could tie it underneath the washers to make your hanky chute look more realistic.

DISAPPEARING PENCIL

YOU NEED
- A handkerchief
- A pencil

Place the handkerchief on the table with one of its corners pointing towards you. We will call this nearest corner 'A' and the one pointing away from you 'B'.

Lay a pencil on the handkerchief. The positioning of the pencil is quite important – it should be as in the picture (1), just a little above the centre of the handkerchief.

Lift corner A and fold it up to just above corner B (2). Now roll the pencil in the handkerchief (3). Keep rolling until corner B comes out from beneath the handkerchief (4). Keep your hands over the middle of the handkerchief so your audience do not see this happen.

Keep rolling for just a little bit more and corner B will come over to rest on top of corner A (5).

Now pull corner B gently back towards you to unroll the handkerchief. When you unroll the handkerchief the pencil is now underneath it. It seems that it penetrated the material by magic!

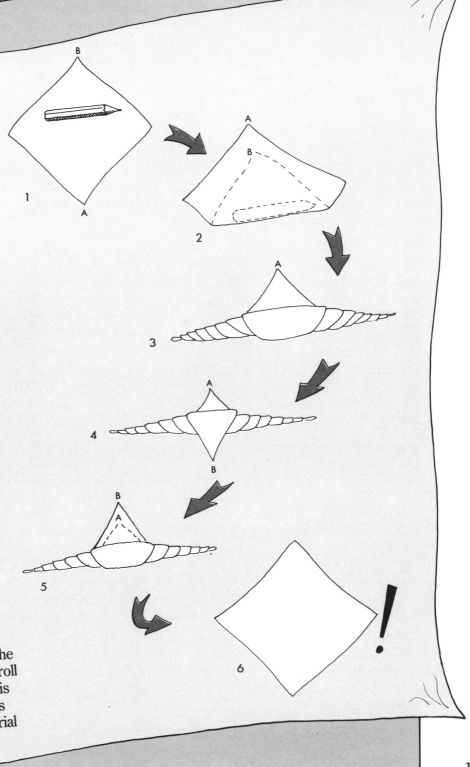

MAGIC NUMBER CARDS

YOU NEED
- Seven pieces of card, or paper
- A pen or pencil

Make a set of cards like the ones shown in the picture. Hand someone the cards and ask them to think of any number between 1 and 90, but not to tell you.

They are then to hand you all the cards bearing the number they have chosen.

Even though the other person has not said a word you now know what number they chose.

How do you know? Well, the cards are specially designed so that all you have to do is add together the numbers at the top left corner of all the cards given back to you. Your total will be the number being thought of by your friend.

If by any chance this trick should go wrong it is because your friend has not given you all the cards bearing his chosen number, or because he has given you cards that do not bear his chosen number, or because you have added up wrongly.

If it does go wrong for any of these reasons simply blame the spectators for not concentrating hard enough – and then try it again with someone else.

32	40	48	56
33	41	49	57
34	42	50	58
35	43	51	59
36	44	52	60
37	45	53	61
38	46	54	62
39	47	55	63

64	71	78	85
65	72	79	86
66	73	80	87
67	74	81	88
68	75	82	89
69	76	83	90
70	77	84	

4	23	46	69
5	28	47	70
6	29	52	71
7	30	53	76
12	31	54	77
13	36	55	78
14	37	60	79
15	38	61	84
20	39	62	85
21	44	63	86
22	45	68	87

16	27	54	81
17	28	55	82
18	29	56	83
19	30	57	84
20	31	58	85
21	48	59	86
22	49	60	87
23	50	61	88
24	51	62	89
25	52	63	90
26	53	80	

1	25	47	69
3	27	49	71
5	29	51	73
7	31	53	75
9	33	55	77
11	35	57	79
13	37	59	81
15	39	61	83
17	41	63	85
19	43	65	87
21	45	67	89
23			

8	27	46	73
9	28	47	74
10	29	56	75
11	30	57	76
12	31	58	77
13	40	59	78
14	41	60	79
15	42	61	88
24	43	62	89
25	44	63	90
26	45	72	

2	26	47	70
3	27	50	71
6	30	51	74
7	31	54	75
10	34	55	78
11	35	58	79
14	38	59	82
15	39	62	83
18	42	63	86
19	43	66	87
22	46	67	90
23			

TUMBLING TUMBLERS

YOU NEED
● Three tumblers, or cups

1. Place the three tumblers on a table. The one in the middle is the right way up, and the other two are placed mouth down.
2. Using both hands, turn over the two tumblers that are on the left.
3. Now cross your arms, pick up the tumblers at each end of the row and turn them both over.
4. Turn over the two tumblers on the left – and all the tumblers will now be mouth upwards.
   Learn these movements so you can do them quickly and without thinking.
5. Having done this in front of your friends, you now turn the centre tumbler mouth down and challenge someone to do what you did – turn the tumblers over two at a time and after three moves have all the tumblers standing the right way up.

No matter how well your friends watched you they will not be able to duplicate your feat – because it just cannot be done. The reason is that their starting position is different to the one you had.

ALL THE SAME

YOU NEED
● Paper and pencil
● A calculator

On a piece of paper you write the number 12345679. (Notice that the 8 is missing). You now ask someone to choose any number from one to nine. Let us assume that three is chosen.

Then you ask that person to multiply the number 12345679 by 27 (it is a good idea to have a calculator handy). Much to everyone's surprise the answer is made up only of the number she chose – in this case the answer is 333333333.

The secret lies in the number you give to multiply the large number. Whatever number from one to nine is chosen, you multiply the chosen number by nine and that is the number you give.

So, if five is chosen you tell the person to multiply the large number by 45 (5×9) and the answer will be all 5s.

Here are the answers for the chosen numbers one to nine:

$12345679 \times 9 = 111111111$
$12345679 \times 18 = 222222222$
$12345679 \times 27 = 333333333$
$12345679 \times 36 = 444444444$
$12345679 \times 45 = 555555555$
$12345679 \times 54 = 666666666$
$12345679 \times 63 = 777777777$
$12345679 \times 72 = 888888888$
$12345679 \times 81 = 999999999$

THE BROKEN PRESENT

YOU NEED
- Pieces of broken china
- A box
- Some wrapping paper

Put the pieces of china into the box. Seal the box and then wrap it in the paper.

Next time it is someone's birthday you show the box and say that it is a birthday present. You go to hand it to your friend but accidentally (on purpose) drop it as you are handing it over.

The box will fall to the floor with a horrible crash. Pick up the box and shake it. The sound of the broken china inside will convince your friend that you really have broken his present.

When you have had a good laugh at your friend's expense you let him out of his misery by explaining that it was all a joke – and then give him his real present (make sure you do not drop it!).

Gift Wrapped

YOU NEED
- An old potato
- Lots of wrapping paper

This is a very old joke, but it is still good for a laugh on someone's birthday.

Wrap the potato in a sheet of paper. Then wrap that in another sheet of paper. Wrap that in yet another sheet of paper – and so on, and so on, and so on.

By the time you have finished there will be no more paper left in the house and your parcel will have grown to quite a size. Wrap it up in some attractive wrapping paper.

Give this to someone as a birthday present – then sit back and have a good laugh as your friend spends ages unwrapping all the layers of paper. He will be quite disappointed when, after all his efforts, he ends up with a mouldy potato – so make sure you have his real present handy to cheer him up.

BETWEEN BOTTLES

YOU NEED
- Two bottles
- A banknote
- A coin

Stand one bottle on a table. Place the banknote on top of the bottle and then invert the other bottle on top of that. Finally, balance a coin on the edge of the base of the uppermost bottle. The complete set-up should look like the illustration shown here.

Ask someone if they can now remove the note without touching either of the bottles and without causing the coin to topple off.

This is another one of those stunts where your friends will have difficulty in solving the problem but you, of course, can do it every time. To do it you take hold of the longer end of the note in one hand. Now hit the note sharply with the forefinger of the other hand. With a bit of luck, and with some practising in private beforehand, the note will slip out from between the bottles.

NOTE AND BOTTLE

YOU NEED
- A small piece of paper, or a banknote
- A bottle

Put the paper, or banknote, on the table and stand the inverted bottle on top of it.

The problem is similar to the one before – you have to get the paper out from under the bottle without touching the bottle.

This one will certainly cause your friends to scratch their heads, but there are actually several ways in which the problem can be solved.

If you pound the table several times with your fist the bottle will gradually move off the paper. This may take a little while so you can speed things up by pulling the paper gently as you are hitting the table.

It is also possible to remove the paper by giving it a short, sharp tug. You should practise this method before showing it to anyone, however, as there is a knack to doing it correctly.

If you pull the note too slowly the bottle will fall over.

The last method is to roll the paper towards the bottle. When the rolled up portion touches the bottle continue rolling and the roll of paper will slowly push the bottle off the paper.

YOU NEED
- A narrow strip of fairly stiff card
- A bottle
- A dried pea or bean, or a small coin

DROP IN THE BOTTLE

Take the card and glue the ends together to form a hoop. Place the hoop on top of the bottle and then put the pea, or coin, on top of the hoop directly over the bottle opening.

You now extend your forefinger and tell everyone watching that you are going to knock the hoop aside and that the pea will drop into the bottle. When you have done this successfully you invite your friends to have a go, but they always fail.

The reason you can do it while your friends are

unsuccessful is that you cheat a little. When you explain what you are going to do you say that you have to hit the hoop on the outside edge, at a point exactly halfway between the top and the bottom (marked X in the picture).

What you actually do is secretly bend your forefinger in as you reach this point, or move it to one side, avoiding point X altogether. Then quickly straighten your finger out again so you actually hit the hoop on the inside of the opposite side (Y) – and the pea drops into the bottle.

When your friends try the stunt by hitting the hoop at X the pea will go flying across the room – so you'd better have a few extra dried peas handy, just in case!

YOU NEED
- A length of rope (about 50 cm)
- A loop of cotton (the same length as the rope)
- A ping-pong ball

ROPE WALKER

Have you ever watched a tightrope walker at the circus or on television and wished that you could do the same? Well, you will not learn how to do it from this book! But you can learn how to train a ping-pong ball to walk across the tightrope!

What! You don't believe it! Well having read other items in this book you ought to know by now that all you need is the secret know-how. The secret know-how for this trick is the loop of cotton. This loop must

be the same length as the rope you are using. It should also be of a dark colour and, for best results, you should wear dark clothing.

Lay the rope and the cotton loop side by side on a table. Now place the ball on the cotton, at its centre.

Now comes the tricky bit. Place your thumbs into each end of the cotton loop and pull it taut. Pick up the rope and the cotton together. To anyone watching it will look as if the ball is on the rope, whereas it is really balanced on the cotton hidden behind the rope.

With practice you will be able to tilt your hands from side to side so that the ball runs back and forth.

CORK THROUGH CORK

YOU NEED
- Two corks, or any small cylindrical objects

Place one cork in the thumb crook of the right hand and the other cork in the thumb crook of the left hand.

Now take hold of the left cork between the forefinger and thumb of the right hand. At the same time grasp the right cork between the forefinger and thumb of the left hand.

All you now have to do is pull your hands apart and the corks will melt through one another. If if did not work there is one simple reason – it's impossible!

But, believe it or not, it can be done – with a bit of trickery. This is how you do it. Position the corks in the crook of each hand as described above. Place the thumb and first finger of your right hand against each end of the cork held in the left hand.

The left hand is twisted away from your body as you go to take hold of the right cork. Your left thumb touches the end of the cork nearest your right palm. At the same time the left forefinger goes under the right thumb to the other end of the cork (the end nearest your body).

This may sound a little complicated but once you get the idea it takes only a fraction of a second to do.

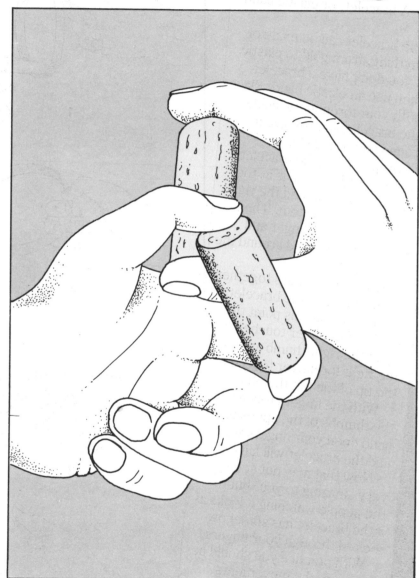

To the people watching it appears that the fingers and the cork are now locked together. To separate the corks is now just a matter of parting the hands. As you do this, turn your hands and it appears that the corks actually melt through one another.

HANDY HINT
You may find this trick easier to do if you use the second finger of each hand rather than the forefingers to hold the corks.

111

YOU NEED
- A bracelet, or elastic band

The bracelet can be made of anything, from gold to plastic. If you don't have a bracelet then use an elastic band. Place both your forefingers inside the bracelet and revolve it round and round (1).

Stop twirling the bracelet when your left hand is at the uppermost point and the right hand is at the bottom. Then quickly loop the finger and thumb of each hand around the bracelet (2).

Bring your fingers together in the centre of the bracelet. It is important at this point that the left forefinger touches the tip of the right thumb and that the right forefinger touches the tip of the left thumb (3).

With the fingers touching the thumbs of the opposite hand open your fingers wide and the bracelet will fall free.

Now that may not seem very amazing to you, but to the people watching it looks as if the bracelet has somehow melted through your fingers.

With practice you should be able to do the movements quite fast, and in one smooth action. This will make the move difficult for your friends to follow and they will probably have great difficulty in duplicating your feat.

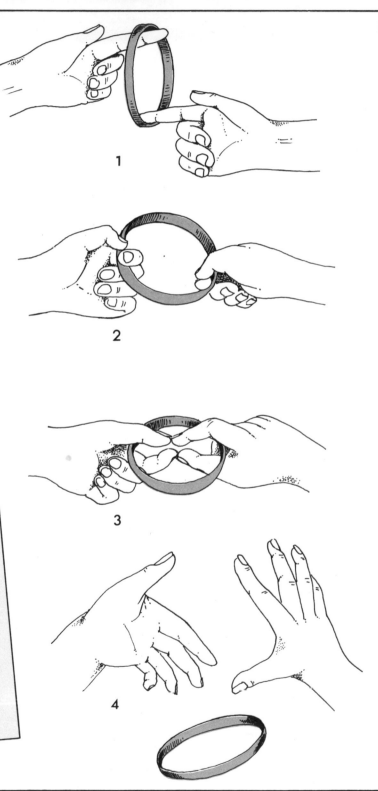

THUMB SPLIT

All you need for this trick is a pair of hands. Before showing it to anyone try it out in front of a mirror so you can see the exact way to hold your hands for best effect.

This is what you do. Hold your left hand out in front of you with the palm facing your body.

Now bend you thumb in towards your body. Place your right thumb alongside the bent left thumb (1).

Put your right forefinger over the place where the two thumbs meet – and from the front it looks fairly normal (2).

Now move your right hand to the right and then back again. It looks as if you have broken your thumb in half and then mended it again (3).

This trick should be done fairly quickly and only when your audience is positioned directly in front of you.

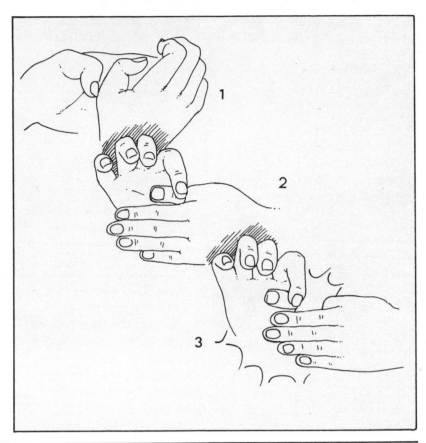

RULER RIDDLE

YOU NEED
● A long ruler

Hold out your forefingers and balance the ruler on them – so that one finger is at one end of the ruler and the other finger is at the opposite end.

Now start moving your fingers slowly towards the centre of the ruler. You will find that first one finger will move and then the other, and they will continue to move alternately until the centre of the ruler is reached!

That is quite a strange thing, but now comes something even stranger. Start to move your fingers apart – and only one finger will move along the ruler! The other stays at the centre!

Provided that you move your fingers slowly this will always happen. Coming from the outside to the centre the fingers will move alternately until they meet at the middle – but moving outwards from the centre only one finger will move to the end of the ruler. Strange, isn't it!

When you have tried it for yourself show your friends and let them have a go.

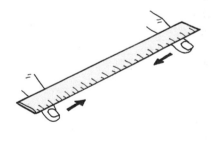

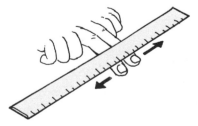

HOW TO MAKE A SHIPS WHEEL

YOU NEED
● A large sheet of paper

You could use a sheet of newspaper for this fantastic demonstration of paper tearing – if you do not mind the print making your fingers dirty.

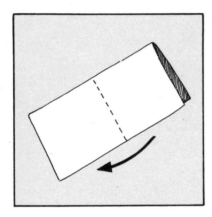

1. Fold the paper in half and hold it with the folded edge at the top. Then fold the paper in half again (as shown by the dotted line in the drawing).

2. Now fold the top left corner down to meet the right edge of the sheet, and fold the paper in half again (bringing edge BC over to edge BD).

3. Turn the paper over completely and then tear or cut out the shapes shown in the drawing.

Open the paper and you should have a super ship's wheel.

Heave ho, me hearties!

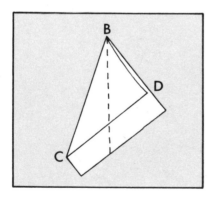

Make a Paper Tree

YOU NEED
● A sheet of paper
● Two elastic bands
● Scissors

Roll the sheet of paper into a tube. To stop the tube from unrolling place an elastic band over each end. Make four cuts in the paper at one end of the tube. Bend out the cut sections.

Now put a finger into the cut end of the tube and pull the paper out from the centre. You now have a remarkable paper tree!

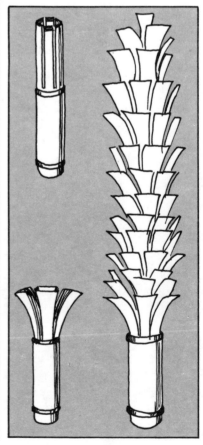

PAPER LADDER

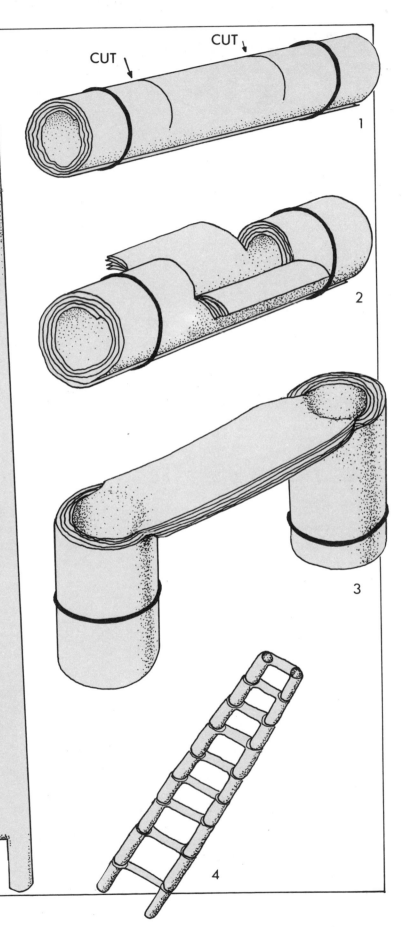

CUT

CUT

1

2

3

4

YOU NEED
- A large sheet of paper or newspaper
- Two elastic bands
- Scissors

Roll the paper into a tube, exactly as you did for the paper tree. Once again, it is a good idea to put an elastic band on each end of the tube to stop the tube unwinding.

1. Now make two cuts in the paper as shown in the illustration. These cuts should go about half-way through the tube.

2. Make a straight cut along the top of the paper between the two cuts and fold down the flaps so formed on each side.

3. Bend the tube at each end so that the paper now forms the shape of a bridge.

Hold the two tubular pieces in one hand and use the other hand to pull the paper out of the two tubes. Be careful that you do not tear the paper as you are doing this.

4. As the paper is pulled upwards it will begin to form the ladder.

POSTCARD LOOP

YOU NEED
- A postcard
- Scissors

Can you make a hole in a postcard big enough for you to put your head through? It sounds impossible – unless you have a very small head. But it can be done. This is how.

Fold the postcard in half lengthways. Now make several cuts down the card as shown by the dotted lines (1).

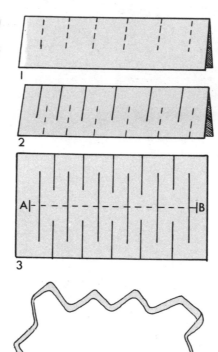

In the picture only a few cuts have been shown, but you should make as many as you possibly can. The more cuts you make the easier the trick is to do.

Next make some more cuts from the opposite edge of the card, as shown by the dotted lines in the picture (2).

Open out the card and it will look like this (3), except, of course, that you will have more cuts in yours. Now, make one last cut from A to B.

Carefully open out the card and it will form into a large loop (4) which will easily go over your head – in fact it may even be large enough to completely go over your body. Now that is magic!

 # MATCH LIFT

YOU NEED
- A matchbox
- A few matches

Open the box and tip the matches on to the table. Move the matches so that they lie neatly side by side, as shown in the picture. The problem you now put to your friends is to get all the matches into the drawer of the box without anyone touching the matches.

Yet another stunt that sounds absolutely impossible and is bound to baffle your friends. You can do it, of course. All you have to do is take the cover of the box in your mouth and then rest it across the matches. Now suck as hard as you can.

Keep sucking as you lift the cover and the matches will cling to it. You now move the matches across to the drawer and position them carefully as you stop inhaling so that all the matches drop into the drawer.

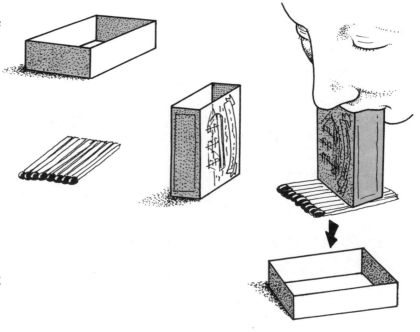

The Tramps and the Chickens

YOU NEED
● Seven matches

Place five matches in a row on the table. Beneath them place two other matches so that the arrangement looks like that in the picture.

Matches 1 to 5 represent five chickens on a farm. The matches marked A and B are two tramps. Now tell your friends a story as you make the following moves.

"Two hungry tramps." Pick up match A in your left hand and B in your right hand.

"One day they came across a farm where there were some chickens in the yard. The first tramp grabbed a chicken." Pick up match 1 in your left hand.

"The second tramp also grabbed a chicken." Pick up match 5 in your right hand.

"The first tramp grabbed another chicken and so did the other tramp." Pick up number 2 in the left hand and number 4 in the right.

"Leaving one chicken for the first tramp." Pick up match 3 in the left hand.

"They were just about to leave the scene of the crime when they heard the farmer

coming. As quickly as they could they put the chickens back in the yard." You now put the five matches back, one at a time, starting with the right hand.

At this point you should have two matches in your left hand and none in the right. Keep your hands closed and your audience will think there is a match in each hand.

"The farmer looked around the yard. When he was satisfied that his chickens were all right he walked back to the farmhouse. This gave the tramps their chance and so they grabbed all the chickens once again." Pick up the five

matches, one at a time, using alternate hands as before. The first match is picked up with the left hand.

"When they got back to their camp they got into a fight because this tramp," raise your closed right fist, "accused this tramp," raise closed left fist, "of being a thief. And he was probably right because this tramp," open right hand to reveal two matches, "had managed to catch only one chicken, but this one had got four!" Open left hand to show that it contains five matches.

"I wonder how he managed that!"

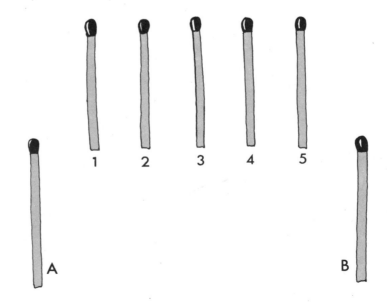

1 2 3 4 5

A   B

117

DOMINO BALANCE

YOU NEED
● A set of dominoes

Have a go at building up a set of dominoes into the structure shown in the picture.

It looks quite amazing and people will think there must be some trick to it. But there is no trickery involved – all you need is a steady hand and some reasonable degree of patience.

You will find it easier to do if you build each platform separately and then carefully, very carefully balance it in position.

It is very likely that the dominoes will fall all over the place the first few times you try this. But keep at it and you'll get there in the end.

Knock it out

YOU NEED
● Eight dominoes

Seven dominoes are formed into the little tower shown in the picture (1).

You now ask someone if they can remove the domino in the centre of the tower, marked X in the illustration, without touching or disturbing any of the others.

To do this you need another domino (but you do not tell your friend that). Place this domino on its edge alongside the tower as shown (2). Now push your forefinger through the bottom part of the tower and press it against the top edge of the extra domino.

This causes the domino to tip up and back to knock out the centre domino as required. It is a good idea to practise this trick a few times first, to get the movement exactly right.

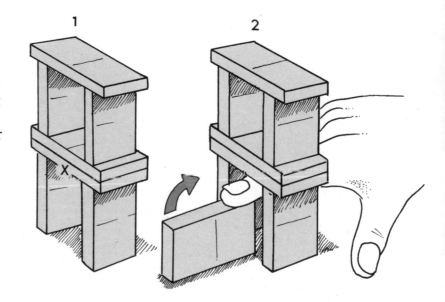

When people see this domino structure on your desk (1) they will wonder how you managed it. But do not tell them. Instead challenge them to do the same.

There is a small secret to achieving success with this building. That is that you use some of the dominoes to provide strategic support while you are doing the building. When the structure is almost completed, these supports are removed and placed on top of the building.

The picture (2) shows the first part of the building, using seven extra dominoes to provide support at the base. The dotted lines at the top show where these dominoes will be placed once the structure is complete. The dotted lines in the final picture (3) show the positions that the supports occupied during the first part of the building.

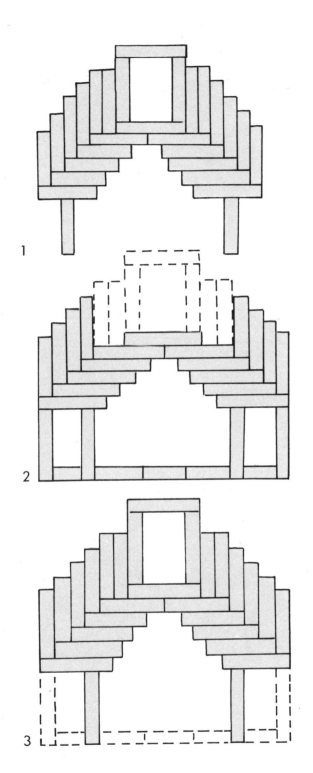

1

2

3

DOMINO BALANCE II

YOU NEED
- A set of draughts, or checkers

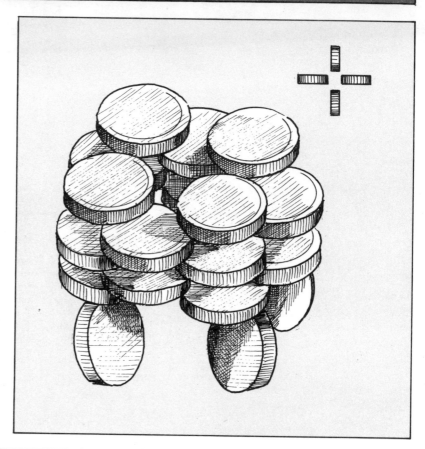

See if you can do this. Take four draughts and stand them on edge on a table-top. Now see if you can stack the other draughts on top of the first four to make a tower like the one shown in the picture.

It is not easy – and it will take a great deal of patience, for they have an annoying habit of dropping all over the place! But it can be done – so keep on trying.

See how many draughts you can stack up before they all fall down. You could even have a competition with your friends to see who can build the highest tower. It should keep you all busy for ages!

MAGIC
MATCHBOX

YOU NEED
- A playing card
- An empty matchbox
- Glue

You show a playing card, wave your hand over it and it changes into a matchbox!

This trick, although quite amazing, is very easy to do. All you need is a special matchbox with a playing card glued to it. The card is glued to one side of the box and then folded over, as shown. A matchbox cover is glued on the back of the card so when it is folded the matchbox appears to be quite ordinary.

Keep the card opened out while you show it to your audience. It looks like an ordinary playing card.

Pass your hand over the card and secretly fold it over. You can now show what appears to be an ordinary matchbox, and there is nothing else in your hands. It seems that you have caused the card to change into a matchbox. It must be matchic!

MAGNETIC CARDS

YOU NEED
- Several playing cards
- A small piece of thin cardboard
- Glue

Just imagine the surprise of your friends when you place several cards on your hand, turn your hand over and the cards do not drop off! The cards appear to be stuck to your hand by magic.

All you need to do this amazing trick is one special card. This has a cardboard tab attached to it, as shown in the picture (1). It is a good idea to use cardboard the same colour as the back of the playing cards so it will not be seen by your friends.

To do the trick you first pick up the special card and place it on your outstretched hand. The tab should go between two of your fingers. Put some more cards on your hand, but make sure that they are tucked under the first card as shown (2).

Now turn your hand over, keeping a tight grip on the tab on the special card and yet another miracle has been accomplished.

If you now let go of the tab all the cards will drop on to your table. Gather them up and hide the special card among the others so no one will know how you managed to accomplish this amazing feat of magic.

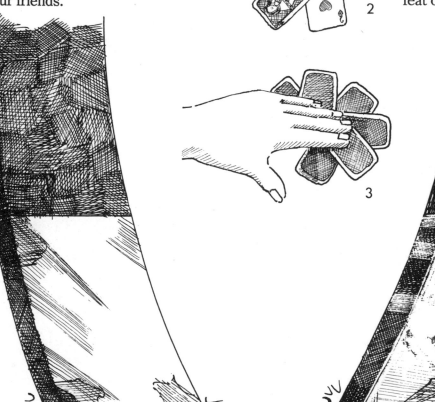

YOU NEED
- A postcard
- A short length of cotton
- Two buttons
- Scissors

Use the scissors to cut a small hole in the postcard, as shown. Above this hole cut two long straight slits in the card. Thread the cotton through the two slits and the hole, and then tie a button to each end of it (the buttons should be larger than the hole).

When you have the opportunity to try this out on your friends simply take this strange device from your pocket and pose the following question, "How can you release the threaded buttons from the card without undoing

BUTTONED UP

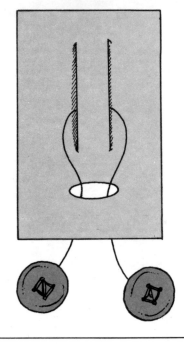

them, cutting the thread, or damaging the card?"

If you have already read further on you will know the answer. But if you have not cheated and are still in the dark just consider the problem for a moment or two.

Do not be too despondent if you have to give up for it is more than likely that your friends will have to give up as well. It is, in fact, impossible – unless you know the secret.

And the secret is this. All you have to do is bend the card in half until you can push the cut portion (between the slits) through the hole. If you now take either one of the buttons and push it through the loop you have just formed the buttons will come free of the card.

BALLOON BLOW

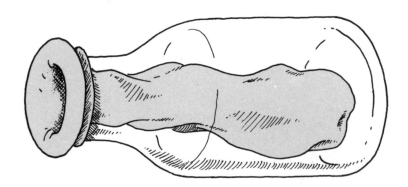

YOU NEED
- A balloon
- A small bottle

Show your friends the balloon and blow it up a little just to show how easy it is. (It is as

well to blow the balloon up a few times before showing this stunt, to make the task of blowing it up in front of your friends that much easier.)

Let the air out of the balloon and push it into the bottle.

Stretch the mouth of the balloon over the top of the bottle opening as shown in the picture.

You now say something like, "You have just seen me blow up this balloon, but I bet none of you can blow up the balloon so that it fills the inside of the bottle."

It looks easy to do, but no matter how much hot air there is inside your friends there is not enough to blow up a balloon inside a bottle. It is absolutely impossible.

Being a clever person you will know that this is all a question of air pressure – but there is no need to tell your friends this.

YOU NEED

- Four playing cards:
  The Queen of Hearts
  The Joker
  Two black number cards
- Scissors and glue

The Vanishing Queen

For this trick you need to make a special card. Cut the Queen of Hearts in half diagonally (1). Glue one half of the Queen on to the face of one of the Clubs or Spades number cards, as shown (2).

Put this card together with the Joker and the second number card and show the three cards face down on a table. Move them around a little so that everyone can see that there are only three cards.

Pick up the cards and hold them with their faces towards you so that no one will see the trick card.

Put the Joker and the number card on top of the special card. Now fan the cards out, but keep the Joker hidden behind the number card so that they appear to be only one card.

You now show the faces of the cards to your audience and it appears that you have a Queen of Hearts between two number cards (3). Tell everyone to keep a careful watch on the Queen.

Close up the fan, turn the cards face down and then spread all three cards out again. Ask someone to point to the Queen. They will naturally point to the centre card. Take out the centre card and place it face down on the table.

Push the other two cards

together so that the Queen on the special card is covered by the other number card. You can now turn these cards face up so everyone will see just

two number cards. The Queen must be on the table, but when that card is turned over it is seen to be a Joker. The Queen has vanished!

123

MATCH A SQUARE

YOU NEED
● Four matches

Place four matches on the table to form a cross like the one shown here.

Can you now form a square? Sounds too simple? Well, it may not be as simple as you think, for you are allowed to move only one match!

The answer is on page 127.

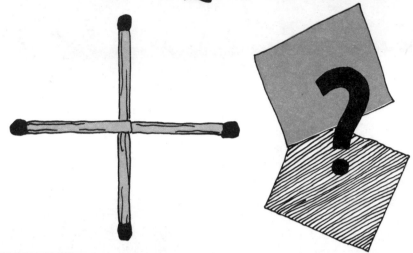

SIXTEEN DOTS AND SIX LINES

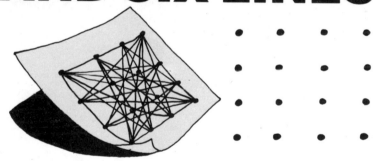

YOU NEED:
● Paper and pencil

On a sheet of paper draw 16 dots in four rows each of four dots.

Without lifting your pen or pencil from the paper, or drawing over any line twice, can you join up all the dots with just six straight lines?

The answer is on page 127.

INSIDE AND OUTSIDE

Show someone a book and say, "I bet I can kiss this book inside and outside without opening it." As you say 'inside' you open the book at any page and as you say 'outside' you tap the cover.

Right, you have made the claim – now, how do you do it?

You kiss the book on the cover then go out of the house and kiss it again. You have done what you said you would do – you have kissed the book inside and outside but you did not open it.

124